CAMP & COTTAGE

BIRDING COLLECTION

THE CRY OF THE
SANDHILL CRANE

By
STEVE GROOMS

NorthWord
PRESS, INC

BOX 1360, MINOCQUA, WI 54548

D1042467

Other volumes in our birding series include:
Bluebirds! by Steve Grooms
The Great Blue Heron by Hayward Allen

Library of Congress Cataloging-in-Publication Data

Grooms, Steve.
     The Cry of the sandhill crane / by Steve Grooms.
         p.   cm. — (Camp & cottage birding collection : 3)
     Includes bibliographical references.
     Summary: Discusses sandhill cranes, especially those along the
Platte River in Nebraska. Contains an appendix with information on
other cranes of the world.
     ISBN 1-55971-142-6 : $16.95
     1. Sandhill crane.   [1. Sandhill crane.   2. Cranes (Birds)]
I. Title. II. Series
QL696.G84G76   1992
598'.31—dc20   91-39399
                                                                          CIP
                                                                          AC

Book design and composition by Cover to Cover Design, Denver, Colorado
Edited by Greg Linder
ISBN 1-55971-142-6

Printed and bound in Singapore

For a free catalog describing NorthWord's line of nature
books and gifts, call 1-800-336-5666.

ACKNOWLEDGMENTS

Though any mistakes in this text are the responsibility of the author, many helpful people did their best to teach me about sandhills and Nebraska's Platte River. Among them, I would like to particularly thank: George Archibald, Bill Dunn, Craig Faanes, Art Hawkins, Carroll Henderson, Rob Horwich, Dayton O. Hyde, Jay Johnson, Doug Johnson, Charles Keller, James Lewis, Gary Lingle, Lonnie and Therese Logan, Steve Nesbitt, Dave Sharp, Scott Swingle, Thomas Tacha, David Thompson, Richard Urbanek, and John Van-DerWalker. Thanks, too, to the anonymous federal researcher whose comments about the efforts to restore whooping cranes were so candid that he/she didn't dare give me his/her name. Finally, I'd like to thank the wonderful people at the International Crane Foundation whose names do not appear above. Your kind patience with me was appreciated.

This book is dedicated to

George Archibald,

John VanDerWalker

and all the other people around

the world who work to improve

the prospects for cranes.

CONTENTS

PREFACE

Steve Grooms and I share a common interest in cranes. For Steve, a critical moment in developing that interest was witnessing the spectacle of hundreds of thousands of sandhill cranes along the dying Platte River.

For me, the critical moment was listening to a Canadian Broadcasting Company radio program for children. In the mid-1950s, in a little one-room white schoolhouse in Nova Scotia, I was enthralled by the CBC dramatization of a pair of whooping cranes that were trying to escape humans so they could successfully nest in the wilderness of northern Canada.

I followed my interest and eventually, together with Ron Sauey, founded the International Crane Foundation, becoming the vernal companion to a mixed-up whooping crane named Tex. Steve, too, followed his interest, and he has created a remarkable book.

In the book, Steve enthusiastically shares a wealth of information about the life history of sandhill cranes and the threats to the Platte River, where some half-million cranes gather in spring to build up fat reserves before their long migration to the arctic. The staging in spring of cranes and several million ducks and geese along the Platte is a wildlife extravaganza that matches the migration of the wildebeest on the Serengeti.

The waters of the Platte have been greatly reduced by upstream damming and diversion projects. If this trend continues, the Platte may soon be dry, and migratory birds may be forced to drink from polluted stock ponds rife with avian cholera. The "crane river" is an international treasure whose destiny rests in the hands of the people of the United States of America.

I invite you to read about the sandhill cranes and their river, and then to join us in becoming involved and in making a difference.

George Archibald
Director
International Crane Foundation

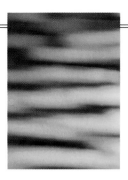

CRANE EVENING

Lonnie Logan pilots his Blazer down the entrance ramp onto I-80 and heads west through the outskirts of Grand Island, Nebraska. The sun on this unseasonably warm March afternoon is low, perhaps two hours above the horizon. Because I am sitting where Lonnie's wife Therese should be, she is curled up with the spare tire in the back of the Blazer. Lonnie's parents, Rex and Mary, occupy the back seat.

I'm here through an extraordinary act of generosity. Lonnie wanted this Monday evening to be a quiet family gathering on the Platte River. The last thing he needed was for a stranger to call, requesting help in observing cranes. Yet so deeply is Lonnie devoted to his twin passions—cranes and the Platte—that he couldn't turn away a sincerely interested person, even today.

Lonnie isn't merely tired. He's bushed. Each year, the town of Grand Island celebrates a "Wings Over the Platte" weekend. The three-day program includes crane seminars, river tours, banquets, wildlife art exhibits and conservation workshops. Lonnie chaired this year's "Wings Over the Platte," so he has just finished hosting about a thousand weekend guests. Now he looks like someone who has been in combat too long. Lonnie has what soldiers call the thousand-yard stare.

We are headed for a duck blind along the Big Bend stretch of the Platte, west of Grand Island. Lonnie tells me the Big Bend is the most pristine remaining area of the river, the stretch most resembling the original Platte.

Each year, thousands of sandhill cranes funnel into this area from far-flung wintering sites throughout the American Southwest and Mexico. They "stage" here, lingering in Nebraska for about six weeks before resuming their northward journey. The spring sandhill get-together on the Platte is the most spectacular congregation of cranes in the world.

I ask Lonnie how he became involved with cranes.

"I've always been an avid outdoors person and waterfowl hunter. When we moved to Grand Island, it was inevitable that I'd spend a lot of time on the river. I just fell in love with the cranes. The bird makes a connection to something far bigger than we are, and you sense something primeval in them. Spending time with cranes is a spiritual experience for us."

"You miss the cranes when they aren't here," Therese adds. "I start looking for that first crane in January. I don't usually see it until sometime in February, but I'm looking."

We begin seeing cranes as soon as the Blazer clears town. Indeed, they're omnipresent. Flocks trade back and forth across the skies. Virtually every field is alive with cranes. They glide between the stubble rows of last fall's corn, probing the topsoil for waste grain with their great bills.

Even at a distance, the cranes' red crowns are prominent. Their long, articulated legs remind me of the jointed aluminum poles used to erect tents. Now and then a bird flutters upward in an explosion of nervous energy, a small sample of the "dancing" for which the birds are famous. In every group of birds, a few high-headed cranes stand sentry, their bodies tense with concern.

The birds are more than just wary. They seem almost paranoid, particularly toward people who pay too much attention to them. The sandhills ignore nearby grazing cattle, and even seem unconcerned about humans who mind their own business. But when a person focuses too much attention on the cranes, the sandhills nervously withdraw toward the center of the section.

A woman in a broad straw hat attempts a clumsy sneak toward a group of about twenty birds. A tall crane on the near edge of the flock slams his bill into the ground, then tosses his head defiantly high. The stylized violence of the gesture stops the crane watcher in her tracks. She probably doesn't realize that these cranes were hunted as legal game in Texas just four weeks ago. Their fear of humans and vehicles is based on recent and bitter experience.

A flock of cranes spirals out of the sky to drop into an old milo field. The birds float groundward, looking like dandelion seeds—a broad mass of wings above, the stilt-like legs dangling

A sandhill stands sentry while others feed.

below. Each bird judiciously spills wind from its cupped wings in order to descend under control. Just before landing, a crane adopts a "flaps down" wing posture, then backstrokes while running a step or two. It is surely bad manners for one crane to plummet onto the head of another. In these crowded fields, each crane must observe precise landing protocol.

Many cranes are gathered in large flocks, but quite a few stand in distinct small groups.

"See those three birds together?" asks Lonnie. "And those over there? Those are families—a pair of adults and a juvenile from last year's nesting. Three birds—that's the normal crane family. In a few weeks, the adults will push the young away so they can concentrate on this season's nesting. But not just yet."

We hear cranes as much as see them. The sound of a sandhill is at once appealing and unearthly. It is, as Lonnie says, primeval, a spooky voice from an unimaginably distant time. The voice of the crane is older than the river itself.

If you've never heard sandhills, imagine a Scotsman clearing his throat in a long, burred *garooo!* into a rain barrel. Depending on your fancy, this burbling

hoot can sound hopeful, mournful, weird, archaic, or simply beautiful. Had the producers of early dinosaur films possessed a little more imagination, they would have given their rubber reptiles the voices of sandhill cranes.

We drive on toward the sun, paralleling the Platte. Because of the trees, we cannot see the river.

As Interstate 80 runs along the Platte, it often overlaps the historic Platte River Road. And with good reason, as this is the most sensible place to put a road. Platte is French for "flat," a faithful translation of the Omaha Indian word "Ne-brath-ka." The French were far more likely to respect Indian place names than were other Europeans, and the name fits. This country was once the floor of a shallow pre-glacial sea. As local people like to say, it is "pancake flat."

The Forty-Niners, Mormons, and other emigrants whose sweat-flecked oxen pulled covered wagons along this same route appreciated level ground. Where Lonnie cruises a mile a minute, pioneer wagons struggled to make 20 miles a day. To the driver of vehicles

Descending, the crane looks like a dandelion seed—a broad mass of wings with legs dangling below.

lacking accelerators and effective brakes, flat roads were a godsend.

This route witnessed one of the grandest mass migrations in history. A third of a million travelers passed this way between 1841 and 1866, in snaky columns of canvas-topped wagons. Through a quirk of history, the Santa Fe Road and the Oregon Trail live in memory, while the Great Platte River Trail does not. Yet this was *the* trail, the single most important westward corridor.

Rarely have so many people taken such a leap of faith, armed with so little reliable information. Pioneers gathered on the extreme western edge of civilization in their time, then plunged headlong into *terra incognita*, the "Great American Desert" lying between them and the land of their dreams. Wave after wave of emigrants trusted hard work and the grace of God to see them across the mysterious empty heart of the nation.

Not all of them made it. Accidents, Cheyenne raiding parties, buffalo stampedes, rattlesnakes, and violent prairie storms took many lives. Of all the trailside scourges, none engendered so much horror as cholera. One of every 17 emigrants who set out on the trail

The typical crane family consists of two adults and a juvenile.

did not survive to celebrate its end. Graves lie ten to the mile along the Great Platte River Road.

Although the emigrants left us a remarkable body of journals describing their adventures, none apparently mentioned the grandeur of the sandhill cranes that stage along the Platte every spring. At first blush, that omission seems to defy logic, for the pioneers were fascinated by western wildlife.

Apparently a scheduling incompatibility kept the emigrants from meeting the cranes. Both the cranes and the pioneers were migrating populations making a dangerous passage. Both were obliged to respect timetables established by inexorable physical realities.

Then, as now, cranes could not fly north until spring's warmth reached their arctic breeding grounds, thawing the soil and stirring insects into activity. Nor could they linger along the Platte beyond early April, lest they arrive north too late to rear their young to sufficient maturity for fall's return trip. The window of opportunity for arctic-nesting birds is small.

Similarly, wagons couldn't roll along the Platte until early April, when there would be fresh grass to fuel the animals that pulled the loads. Yet to tarry was to risk a snowy death in the high Rockies in fall, the fate that befell the infamous Donner Party in 1846.

Each year the pioneer trains embarked upon their transcontinental adventure just as vast flocks of grey cranes were lifting off the Platte to complete their northward journey. Two massive migrations flowed through this small region without intersecting, because they could have met only if one group or the other was fatally off-schedule.

Lonnie explains that three subspecies of sandhills come here: the lesser, the Canadian, and the greater sandhill. "Mostly what you're seeing are lessers," he adds. About 80 percent of the world's population of lessers passes through this area each spring.

Collectively, the three subspecies of cranes staging along the Platte comprise what is called the mid-continental population of sandhills. The first cranes usually arrive by the middle of February. The peak typically falls in the third week of March, at which time half a million cranes will be packed into 60 miles of river along the Platte and a 20-mile stretch of the North Platte. The last crane leaves around the 20th of April, and the Platte falls strangely silent.

The spectacle of so many cranes attracts an impressive congregation of humans. As Lonnie's Blazer draws close to the Big Bend, we begin passing cars pulled hastily over to the side of the road. People brace elbows on car hoods to steady their binoculars. A few cars have window-mount spotting scopes. Most vehicles sport Nebraska plates, but a surprising number have come from distant states. We pass a Volvo from New Jersey.

Intense interest in these cranes dates back less than two decades. In the early 1970s conservationists fighting the proposed Mid-Continent Irrigation Project began calling attention to the Platte's unique importance for sandhill and whooping cranes. A Roger Tory Peterson book celebrated the Platte's crane gathering as one of the world's grandest ornithological spectacles. Then television discovered the Platte's sandhills and the water-rights conflict they symbolized. Various nature shows have featured the Platte sandhills, including an Audubon special and a segment on CBS's *Sunday Morning* narrated by the avuncular Roger Welsch. With publicity came crowds.

Some crane watchers are casual visitors who roam the gravel roads south of the river until they've seen their fill of birds. Others are serious birders or people fascinated by cranes. For them, coming to the Platte in March is a kind of spiritual pilgrimage, something they must do at least once in a lifetime. About 80,000 crane tourists visited the Platte in 1990. The number has been doubling annually in recent years, and it shows no signs of peaking.

Packing that many humans into one area—even that many gentle, bird-watching humans—inevitably causes problems. Crane watchers perform loopy highway maneuvers while chasing overhead flocks. They pull over at awkward places, creating traffic jams. They block farm driveways with their mini-vans. They tromp paths in the mushy spring soil of private land. And they harass a few cranes at a time when cranes really shouldn't be harassed.

Sandhills spooked off a section of the river will afterward avoid it and its adjacent wet meadow. Though conservationists hope people will come to marvel at the Platte's cranes, they know that clumsy crane watchers frighten some birds and cause them to head north in less than peak condition.

While bird watchers irritate some farmers and spook some cranes, they spend about $15 million each year in local communities. If the "multiplier effect" is taken into consideration, crane tourism has a $45 million impact. The crane watchers' checkbooks and charge cards remind Nebraska businessmen that the destruction of the Platte's crane habitat would have dire economic consequences.

We are seeing more and more cranes. It's impossible to look into a field and not see them. Groups of cranes—three, 13, 130—are everywhere. And from everywhere comes the gurgling *gar-ooo-a-a* of crane music. The crane calls are so frequent that they are no longer a sound, but an acoustic environment.

I ask Lonnie why the cranes come *here*. He smiles. This answer he knows by heart. Lonnie's mind takes a cat nap while his voice runs on autopilot.

"Three reasons. First, they come seeking a safe place to roost. The Platte is the only ecosystem along the whole migrating route that meets all the cranes' requirements for roosting."

"And what are they?"

"Cranes require shallow water, preferably submerged sandbars surrounded by deeper water. They demand areas surrounded by wide open spaces with no vegetation. Sandhills prefer to have a 2,000-foot wide open space around their roosts, though they'll use areas where vegetation is as close as 500 to 1,000 yards away. All that water and space gives them security against predators.

"Second, they need to put on from 20 to 25 percent of their body weight in fat while they're here. There will be no food when they arrive up north. The journey and the duties of nesting put tremendous demands on their bodies, so they simply must build up reserves here. They get that from waste corn in grain fields.

"Third, the cranes need the wet meadow complexes that lie adjacent to the Platte. They used to be the cranes' primary feeding ground. Those areas supplied calcium and protein and minerals needed to trigger the breeding process."

Frowning, Lonnie adds, "The birds have lost as much as 90 percent of the wet meadows to irrigation and water projects. They can't afford to lose *any* more."

Lonnie turns the Blazer down a gravel road. We cross two rattly bridges over what seem like ordinary farm-country rivers but are actually channels of the Platte. Lonnie points out farms on the table-flat flood plain between

The lesser crane.

the river branches. "That used to be crane habitat, wet meadow. Now, because of reduced river flows, it has gone to agricultural development."

We turn down a dirt lane through a privately owned field. When the Blazer halts beside a barbed wire fence, we free Therese from the vehicle's back end.

"It's a short walk now," says Lonnie. "From here on we need to speak quietly, to avoid spooking the cranes."

On this warm spring day, the river has a ripe smell. The rich, black earth has been soaking up solar heat all day. The juices of life have returned to the mud. Fragile shoots of grass rise like green hairs from the areas receiving the most spring sunlight.

We walk through a phalanx of willows and cottonwoods growing densely along the river. Were we to take a chain saw to the largest of these and examine the stump, it would contain about 40 annular rings. These are "Kingsbury trees," trees that were able to establish a firm grip on life only after the Kingsbury Dam began depleting river flows in 1950. Before then, torrential spring meltwater floods and ice flows flushed away all young vegetation before it could take root.

Lonnie's duck blind lies half-buried

From a duck blind near the river's edge, Lonnie Logan "fools around" with his camera.

in the sand near the river's edge, facing north. "We spend a lot of time here," Lonnie muses. "Mostly fooling around with cameras. But it's a good spot for hunting, too." Feathers in the sand indicate that someone plucked a Canada goose here ·last fall. A derelict mallard decoy with a vapid expression lies cocked on its side.

A surprisingly broad channel of the Platte runs by from the west, on our left. Something is odd about the currents here. They curl and diverge in complex patterns as they glide over the shallow sandbars that I now begin to detect.

Sandhills roost on these sandbars each night. At daybreak, they leave to feed in the adjacent grasslands, then move to the grain fields to glean grain, dance, and preen their feathers. The cranes grab a second load of corn late in the afternoon before returning at dusk to the safety of the Big Bend's shallow sandbars.

Off to the east, we see immense flocks of cranes winging low along the horizon like jabbering plumes of smoke. Unlike the migrating sandhill flocks I have seen soaring lazily high above the prairie in fall, these birds flap their wings with an air of purpose.

At sunrise on the Platte a crane dance has begun for these early risers.

Other birds are here, too. Barking like dogs, a pack of snow geese goes by. Mergansers paddle lazily in the current. A flock of mallards, handsome in climax plumage, beats across the evening sky. Lonnie points out a bald eagle, a bird that probably shares Lonnie's interest in ducks. Eagles are fairly common along the Platte in winter. Two teal fire past us like something shot from a catapult.

In all, about 300 species of migratory birds use the Platte seasonally, about 125 of them nesting here. Waterfowl stage here when the spring flows are highest. Later, when more sandbars are exposed, the Platte hosts nesting shore birds, such as the endangered piping plover and the least tern.

"What's that duck?" Lonnie asks Therese.

"Pintail."

"Right!" Lonnie is surprised.

"Lonnie thinks I don't know pintails," Therese explains. "So when he asks about a duck, I say pintail." Therese may not know pintails, but she certainly knows Lonnie.

◆ ◆ ◆

Cranes sweep over us in increasing

Cranes preen and loaf in a midday meadow roost.

numbers. They seem to be landing on submerged sandbars not far downstream from the duck blind, although we can't see them. Some come by in ragtag formations, others in energy-efficient chevrons. One flock swings by at low altitude.

"You hear that?" Lonnie asks. "That high-pitched call is a juvenile. Adults have lower voices." Just as humans do, sandhills experience an adolescent voice change. This happens when the juvenile crane is about 11 months old, so these young cranes are soon to experience the switch-over.

From a distance, cranes sound much alike. But we can hear individual voices within low-flying flocks. The calls seem to differ in duration, pitch, and urgency. A single crane flies by just above the river, crying plaintively. I wonder if this is a juvenile separated from its parents—one lonely young bird seeking familiar voices in the cacophony of 500,000 bugling cranes.

Still more cranes come, some so low that we can hear the sibilant sound of their wings like luffing sails. Because the light is failing, the cranes that pass us now are dark silhouettes against a taffy-colored prairie sunset. The flow of cranes is almost constant. Yet the sight is not as potent as the sound. It seems that as the rheostat controlling the sunlight is turned down, the volume control on the crane cries is cranked up to a tumultuous level.

Therese leaves the blind to sit silently and absorb the scene. This is her first evening on the river this year, her first communion with the cranes. Rex and Mary shake their heads in disbelief at the tumult of the downriver cranes.

At one point I tilt my head back, staring straight into the sky, and it occurs to me that most of the world's population of sandhill cranes is flying directly overhead, each bird with a tummy full of soggy corn. I flip up the hood on my parka, just in case.

The din of crane music increases to an almost frightening level. I had expected many birds. I had expected a great deal of calling. But nobody could have prepared me for the acoustic impact of half a million cranes all trumpeting at once through their long tracheas.

In all of North America, only a handful of animal calls have the power to stir the human soul as profoundly as these crane cries. The yodeling of loons on a northwoods lake, the bugling of elk across a misty meadow, the lugubrious howling of a wolf pack in a wilderness forest—these are sounds that bypass the ears to sink their teeth into a nerve deep within the listener, these and the ancient gurgling cries of cranes echoing over a dark river.

Birds begin populating the sandbars closer to us, but the light this evening

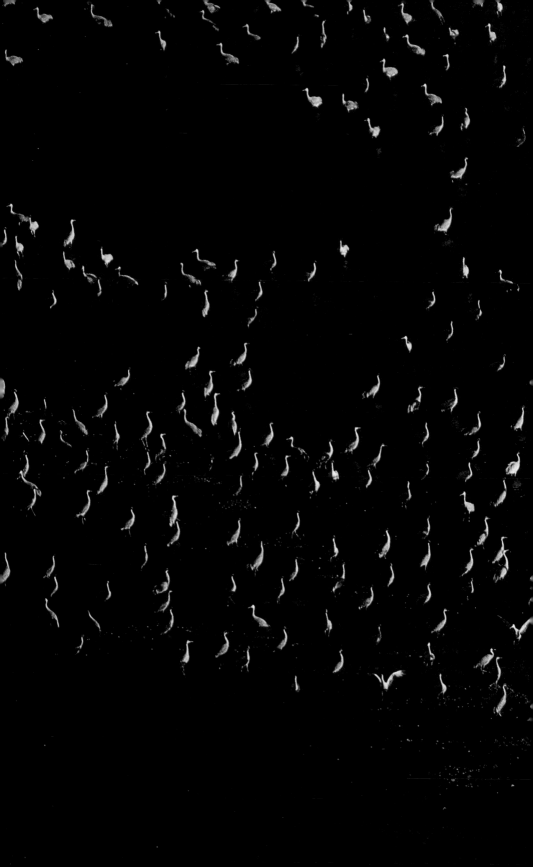

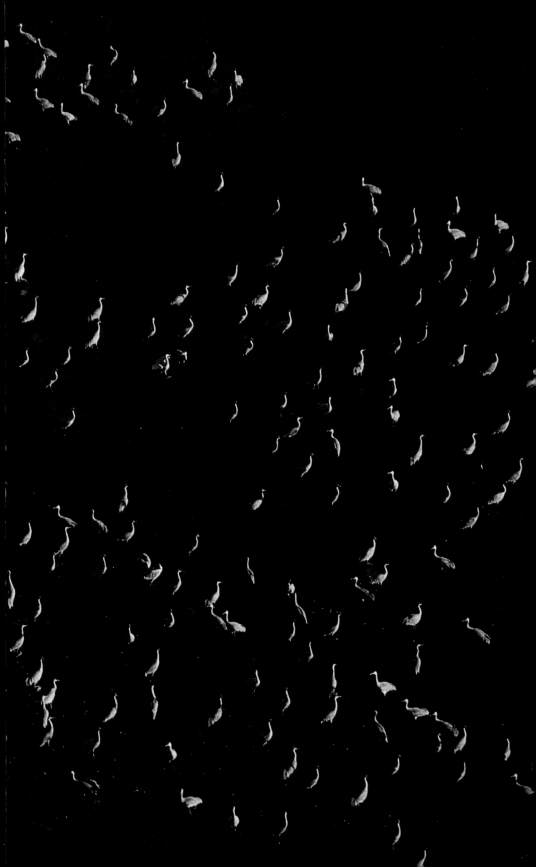

will not let us see them. The sun has become an incandescent pumpkin with fuzzy edges. It begins sliding down below the bank-side willows. Upstream, the twisting currents of the Platte reflect the golden sky like a sheet of hammered metal. We could see cranes against that light if any were there, but downstream where the cranes gather everything is an indigo murk.

I can imagine what the roosting birds look like from what I have read. According to some accounts, cranes space themselves as if positioned on a grid of four-foot squares, each bird staying just beyond the reach of its neighbors' sharp bills. Seen from the air, the oval flocks reveal the shape of submerged sandbars with the precision of a hydrographic map.

Many cranes stand on a single leg while roosting. This inspired the ancients to believe that cranes slept while holding a stone clutched in one foot. If startled, the crane would drop the stone and alert the rest of the flock. We know that's not true, but scientists remain puzzled about why cranes, flamingoes, and similar birds choose to stand on one leg.

And picture this: Occasionally, a crane will drop into the river and allow the current to tumble it along for several feet. This odd behavior is infectious. When one crane takes a water slide, others nearby are inspired to copy it. Nobody knows why cranes do this.

Perhaps because it's a fun way to bathe.

"Damn!" says Lonnie. "Something spooked them." The crane cries have risen in pitch and intensity, becoming a thunderous crescendo that's almost painful to hear. I think I have heard this stunning sound before. Memory finally clicks: This is the roar of frenzied teens as the Beatles appear onstage at the Los Angeles Coliseum! Crane calls fill the darkness until they form an almost palpable wall of sound.

Now the sun is totally gone. The crane chorus becomes less frantic, yet closer. The birds have apparently filled up the lower river and are taking up roosts near the blind. Staring through the velvety light, at last I can make out the hazy silhouettes of tall grey birds moving on the sandbars before us like fitful ghosts under a Cheshire Cat moon.

"They're getting too close!" hisses Lonnie.

And so five crane watchers sneak away from the duck blind, silent and bent at the waist. We go furtively through the willows like cat burglars, and the only things we disturb are cottontails romping in the young grass along the Platte.

Behind us, cranes bicker and grumble, demanding elbow room. Crane families make reassuring "I'm right here, are you still there?" calls to each other. I smile, imagining them bidding each other goodnight in the dark, like television's Waltons. "Goodnight, Mama. Goodnight, Papa."

"Goodnight. Go to sleep now, Crane-Boy."

The individual and collective *gar-ooo-a-as* subside to a murmur. One crane after another decides it has found a safe place, relaxes, and succumbs at last to sleep.

EMISSARIES FROM A DISTANT AGE

WHAT IS A CRANE?

Cranes resemble such tall, leggy, long-necked birds as storks, flamingos, egrets, and herons. Yet in spite of physical similarities, cranes are not closely related to those large wading birds. The similarities result from parallel evolution, a multiple re-invention of the wheel.

The blueprint of a bird configured this way was produced several times in the process of evolution, a fact that is surely significant. Birds shaped more or less like cranes are uniquely suited for life along the marshy transition zone where land meets water. That sloppy, fertile ecotone is one of the safest and most food-rich ecological regions on earth—basically, a good place to live.

In what ways do cranes differ from similar birds?

Storks, because they perch in trees, have the usual three front toes plus a long hind toe enabling them to grasp branches. Storks nest off the ground. Their young are born naked and helpless, remaining in the nest for a long time before venturing into the world. Adult storks are silent.

Flamingos have webbed feet and a ponderous, drooping beak. Flamingos strain mouthfuls of matter through a filter in order to isolate the small marine animals they eat.

Herons and the closely related egrets also have the grasping hind toe for perching in trees. They typically nest

---

A Florida sandhill crane: Despite appearances, it's not closely related to storks, flamingos, egrets, or herons.

in colonies. When a heron walks, its neck has a noticeable crook, even when the bird extends it. In the air, a heron carries its neck folded in a tight loop against the body. Herons feed by stalking the shallows to spear fish.

In all respects, cranes differ from these apparently similar birds. Cranes generally appear taller and more graceful than other large waders. Their heads are more delicate relative to their bodies. In most crane species, the hind toe is short, elevated, and of no use for grasping. Cranes can perch in trees, yet it doesn't come naturally to

them and few crane species do it. Cranes are ground-nesters whose young quickly become mobile. They're gregarious at most times, but they nest in isolated pairs rather than rookeries. Unlike herons, cranes walking on the ground have straight necks. They carry their necks straight and extended in flight. Whereas herons mainly eat fish and live on the wet side of the marshy land/water border, cranes are mainly vegetarians well-suited for life on the dry side of the marshy shoreline.

North America has only two cranes—the sandhill and the highly

Above: An overview of the Platte, the sloppy, fertile zone that serves as home to half a million cranes each spring.

endangered whooping crane. Cranes inhabit all continents of the world except South America.

THE SIGNIFICANCE OF CRANES

Mankind has always associated the crane with the loftiest and most appealing of spiritual values. To a number of cultures, cranes have represented fidelity, longevity, good fortune, insight, the love of peace, beauty, vigilance, and nobility. The veneration of cranes runs especially deep in the Orient, but societies from many different centuries and geographical regions have regarded cranes with unique respect and affection. The cranes of myth and legend are unfailingly compassionate, wise, and loving.

There are some fairly obvious reasons why humans have been so inspired by cranes. Cranes are among the world's largest birds, some standing as tall as an adult human. Like humans, they walk upright on two legs. Like humans, cranes dance. Cranes, in fact, are considered the most accomplished dancers in the animal kingdom. Their stylized acrobatics have inspired human imitators in Africa, Australia, the Orient, and the American Southwest. In many folk legends, dancing ladies are mysteriously transformed into cranes . . . or cranes into ladies.

Even in very early times, people apparently understood that cranes mate for life and live longer than most birds. Inevitably, cranes became symbols for marital fidelity and longevity. In traditional Japanese weddings, the bride's kimono features a crane lovingly stitched in lustrous threads, to symbolize the hope that this marriage will have the endurance of a union between cranes.

"Congruence," from *grus*, is one of several words in the English language deriving from the contemplation of cranes. It's a congenial word, meaning "the quality of agreeing or coinciding." No word better sums up the significance of cranes to humans. Cranes excel at establishing stable families and forming lasting bonds. Cranes have a genius for making things come together harmoniously.

Even modern science, whose cold fish-eye has stripped so many animals of their mysteries, can't reduce cranes to ordinariness. Through science, we learn that cranes have been here on earth for about 60 million years, which makes them our living bridge to the inscrutable past. Early cranes may have foraged while keeping a wary eye cocked on nearby dinosaurs and dining on plants that have long since disappeared from earth.

Conservationist Aldo Leopold was thrilled by the ancient origins of cranes. In his nature classic, *A Sand County Almanac*, he writes:

The crane stitched into a Japanese wedding kimono (left) symbolizes a long and harmonious union.

Our appreciation of the crane grows with the slow unraveling of earthly history. His tribe, we now know, stems out of the remote Eocene. The other members of the fauna in which he originated are long since entombed within the hills. When we hear his call we hear no mere bird. He is a symbol of our untamable past.

Cranes were ancient before the glaciers were young. Cranes soared above the clouds when the Rocky Mountains were newly minted; before many present-day rivers were formed; and long before the first beetle-browed early humans left the trees to forage on the plains of Africa.

Leopold writes:

And so they live and have their being—these cranes—not in the constricted present but in the wider reaches of evolutionary time. Their annual return is the ticking of the geologic clock. Upon the place of their return they confer a peculiar distinction . . . a paleontological patent of nobility, won in the march of aeons.

THE ANCIENT, SUCCESSFUL SANDHILL

North America's only common crane is the sandhill. Were it not for sandhills, only a handful of Americans would ever have seen a crane. But sandhills flourish. They have given thousands of people their only personal experience of the crane family's unique beauty and mystery. Sandhills have recently been enlisted in the battle to protect endangered crane species around the world. Because it's abundant, the sandhill is the perfect test species for developing techniques to help crane species that have fallen on hard times.

Sandhills also play a crucial role in the fight to save one of America's great

western rivers. In the early 1970s, an acrimonious debate arose over an ambitious irrigation project that threatened Nebraska's Platte River, a river already being bled to death by water withdrawals. Conservationists rushed to educate the public about the unique importance of the Platte to the world's largest population of sandhill cranes. People who can't identify emotionally with a *river* readily identify with the lovely birds that have danced along the shores of the Platte for as long as it has been there.

As the oldest living bird species, the species that can claim the longest successful tenure on earth, the sandhill holds a pre-eminent position in the world of birds. A sandhill's fossil wing bone was found in Nebraskan deposits dating back nine million years, so sandhills have been citizens of North America for at least that long. American cultural biases may lead us to suspect that a species so old must be primitive and is probably somewhat dysfunctional. But the opposite is true. Extended longevity is the ultimate honor that evolution grants a species, and sandhills are therefore the most-favored survivors of the bird world.

The sandhill comes to us today as an emissary from an ancient and largely unknowable age. We owe it the respect due a time traveler whose eerie yellow eyes have witnessed the birth and death of glaciers and the innumerable scramblings of the North American species.

Aldo Leopold understood the significance of cranes perhaps better than any contemporary American. He writes:

Our ability to perceive quality in nature begins, as in art, with the pretty. It expands through successive stages of the beautiful to values as yet uncaptured by language. The quality of cranes lies, I think, in this higher gamut, as yet beyond the reach of words.

THE SIX SANDHILLS

Sandhill crane researchers contend with unusual challenges. Their subjects are among the wariest birds in North America. Sandhills nest in some of the most remote terrain on earth, selecting locations where they can easily spot any approaching predator or snoopy biologist. And the cryptic color of sandhills has been described as "one of Nature's triumphs of protective coloration." All of this makes sandhills difficult to observe.

Identifying sandhills while observing them can be even trickier. Except for indiscernible differences in size, males and females are virtually identical. And from the time they are several months old, the juveniles closely resemble their parents and aren't much smaller.

More complications arise from the fact that the sandhill is not a single bird, but six subspecies. The different subtypes sometimes occupy the same habitat at the same time. And if that weren't confusing enough, the six subtypes are dismayingly similar in appearance, with minor differences in—you guessed it—size.

The six subtypes are: the greater, lesser, Canadian, Florida, Mississippi, and Cuban. Collectively, they comprise *Grus canadensis*, the sandhill crane. All are large, impressive birds, standing four to five feet tall with wingspans of six to seven feet.

It isn't terribly unusual for a bird species to have migrating and residential (non-migrating) subspecies, but the clear and absolute difference between sandhill subtypes is unusual. Greater, lesser, and Canadian sandhills *always* migrate. Florida, Mississippi, and Cuban sandhills *never* migrate.

Researchers think that the original North American sandhill was a migrating bird. Even the resident sandhills have some characteristics of migrating birds, such as the pattern of their molt. So it seems likely that the resident birds evolved from a migrating ancestor, rather than the other way around.

Nothing about sandhills is more remarkable than their versatility. A migrating bird is different from a resident bird, but some sandhills travel 7,000 miles a year while others go nowhere at all. It's a long way from Cuba to Siberia, with correspondingly different climates, but some sandhills nest in the vicinity of alligators while others nest among polar bears. The sandhill, then, is not a simple bird.

THE GREATER SANDHILL

Grus canadensis tabida is the largest sandhill. Males weigh about 12 pounds, females about 9 1/2 pounds. There are legends of a few grain-fattened males nudging the scales to 15 pounds in fall.

Greater sandhills nest in a broad band between the fortieth and forty-fifth parallel (as far south as northern Illinois to as far north as Vancouver Island). They build their nests in or near shallow marshes, often those located in arid grasslands or refuges that are rarely disturbed by humans.

The four major flocks of greater sandhills cover different ranges. The Great Lakes flock nests in Minnesota, Michigan, Wisconsin, and parts of southern Canada. This flock winters in central Florida. There are no major concentrations during the spring migration, but in fall these birds concentrate in massive numbers at the Jasper-Pulaski Game Preserve in northwestern Indiana. The flock has made a strong comeback from low population levels early in the 20th century, and now numbers about 11,000 individuals.

The Rocky Mountain flock nests in eastern Idaho, southwestern Montana, and western Wyoming. A number of these birds breed in Grand Teton National Park. Most Rocky Mountain birds winter in the Rio Grande Valley of New Mexico, particularly in the Bosque del Apache wildlife refuge.

A third flock nests in northwestern Nevada and winters in southern California.

The fourth flock of greaters nests in south-central Oregon and northeastern California, wintering in California's Central Valley. A few additional birds nest on Vancouver Island, but little is known about their movements.

The greater sandhill was classified as

"threatened" for some time but has been moved off the list, primarily because of increases in the Rocky Mountain flock. The national population of greater sandhills is currently about 35,000, of which more than two-thirds are Rocky Mountain birds.

The greater sandhill once bred widely in meadows and marshes throughout the Midwest and West. It has lost more habitat than any other subtype and, though these majestic cranes have staged a comeback in some regions, a great many marshes that used to ring with crane music have been silent for over a century.

THE CANADIAN SANDHILL

Grus canadensis rowani is often called the "intermediate," because that's what it is—an intergrade between the lesser and greater sandhill. Some taxonomists question its distinctness and would lump it in with the lesser. Biologists differentiate Canadians from the lesser and greater through careful measurement of the culmen (upper bill) and tibiotarsus (the longest leg bone). Male Canadians weigh about nine pounds.

The Canadian sandhill breeds in bulrush marshes and muskeg in central Canada, from Great Slave Lake in the Northwest Territories to the southern shores of Hudson Bay and along the western shores of James Bay. Canadians mainly winter along the Gulf Coast of Texas, staging on the Platte River when migrating north.

Researchers know virtually nothing about possible habitat losses for this subspecies, as it has only been recognized for a few decades. The Canadian sandhills appear to be relatively secure, because they nest in desolate tundra regions that humans have not been tempted to develop. A recent "guesstimate" put their numbers at 54,000.

THE LESSER SANDHILL

Grus canadensis canadensis was once called the "little brown crane," though it isn't very little, and it's no browner than other sandhills. The lesser stands almost four feet tall and weighs seven to eight pounds.

This crane has seven-league boots, migrating two or three times as far as other sandhills. Some lessers cross the Bering Strait to nest on the eastern coast of Siberia. Most nest in lonely tundra, marsh, and coastal areas from Alaska all the way to Hudson Bay. Like the Canadian, the lesser rears its young in bogs and muskeg where black flies abound and humans rarely venture.

Lessers winter along the Gulf Coast of Texas, the central valley of California, and the state of Chihuahua in north central Mexico. The heaviest winter concentrations are in New

---

Overleaf: Two Canadian sandhills. The cry of the crane has been ringing forth for some sixty million years.

to a drier habitat than that used by migrating sandhills.

The birds have lost a great deal of habitat in the past, though they have benefited from legislation protecting wetlands and establishing refuges. While the loss of marshland has threatened cranes all over the world, Florida sandhills have been hurt at least as much by the loss of usable upland habitat to human development.

Florida sandhills seem secure. Their numbers haven't increased or decreased significantly in recent years, and there is no reason to fear that they will run into trouble in the near future. It was once thought that these birds enjoyed higher recruitment rates than other sandhills (which means they successfully raise more of their young), but that isn't the case. As a resident bird, the Florida sandhill is spared the high rate of mortality suffered by migrating birds but, on the other hand, it often reproduces at a slightly later age. The population currently numbers about 5,000. The Florida sandhill has proven itself a resourceful, adaptable bird.

THE MISSISSIPPI SANDHILL

One of the first birds to benefit from the 1973 Endangered Species Act was the Mississippi sandhill, the *Grus canadensis pulla*. When conservationists learned that a freeway was to be routed right through a marsh where 40 sandhills were nesting, they sued to alter the project. In 1972, researcher John Aldrich confirmed old suspicions that these birds were Mississippi sandhills, a new sixth subspecies, not "just" more Florida sandhills. The Mississippi cranes thus warranted protection as an endangered species and became the first birds to force the re-routing of an interstate highway.

Two decades later, the Mississippi birds are still rare and endangered, although the cranes were helped by a 1974 Supreme Court decision leading to the creation of the Mississippi Sandhill Crane National Wildlife Refuge.

The flock's population has generally hovered at 40 to 50 individuals. It was increased substantially through a recent release of Mississippi sandhills reared at the federal Patuxent research station in Laurel, Maryland. There, cranes were reared by hand under an experimental protocol that did not cause them to "imprint" on human beings. When 29 of these young cranes were added to the wild Mississippi sandhill flock, they fared extremely well. Months later, 28 were still alive. Researchers hope they have succeeded in developing the right technology for building the numbers of the Mississippi sandhill flock.

The Florida sandhill: A resident bird spared the dangers of migration.

THE CUBAN SANDHILL

Grus canadensis nesiotes clings to existence at three small locations in Cuba: Zapata Swamp National Park (near the Bay of Pigs); the Isle of Pines; and parts of the Camaguey Province. The most recent estimate put the population at just 54 birds. The Cuban sandhill is extremely endangered, due primarily to past indiscriminate shooting and the more recent conversion of Cuban wetlands to agricultural uses.

Concerned Cubans are described as "desperate" to save the bird, but they lack the staff, the funds, and the expertise to accomplish what is needed. Overcrowded and scarce, the Cuban sandhill may become yet another innocent victim of the needs of our expanding human population.

Above: The Mississippi sandhill. Overleaf: Sandhills forage in a corn stubble field near the Platte River.

UNDERSTANDING THE SANDHILL

IDENTIFYING SANDHILLS

Viewed from a distance, adult sandhills appear uniformly grey, with a prominent red crown. The crown, a patch of naked skin, starts at the base of the bill, runs back under the eyes and over the top of the head. The throat and nape are white. The cheeks are white or light grey—a significant distinction to the cranes themselves. The four to five-inch bill is dark grey. The legs and feet are black.

Closer examination reveals varied shadings of color in the body. Lawrence Walkinshaw, the avid crane researcher and sandhill authority, has described sandhills as "light to pale mouse gray with fawn color washed on the feathers of the back, wings, and shoulders." The grey or grey-brown back, wings, and shoulders are noticeably darker than the neck and belly.

An anatomical curiosity about the sandhill is its "tail that is not a tail." Sandhill tails resemble those of Canada geese, but they are visible only when the birds extend their wings. When a crane is on the ground with folded wings, what appears to be the tail is actually an extension of the tertials, the wing feathers closest to the body. This false tail, a flouncy and foppish thing, is often likened to a bustle.

A sandhill chick changes appearance rapidly as it develops. A young chick is a tawny sedge color, and is fluffy. At a few weeks old, the chick resembles a

leggier version of Easter ducklings. When a few weeks older, the leggy chick is called a colt. Why? Aldo Leopold answers: "On some dewy June morning watch them gambol over their ancestral pastures at the heels of the roan mare, and you will see for yourself." Adult male sandhills are, in fact, sometimes called roans, and females are referred to as mares.

The feathers of colts are grey at the base, and sedge or burnt sienna toward the tips. Gradually the grey color prevails much the way the natural shade replaces a dyed color in human hair, moving out from the roots. Through a molting process, young birds gradually acquire the dun grey color of adults.

Juvenile sandhills resemble their parents, but have feathered foreheads. The top of the head from the crown to the nape of the neck is tawny.

THE FLYING SANDHILL

From a distance, flying sandhills often look like a broad pair of wings with no bird attached. The delicate head, slender neck and stick-like legs are dwarfed by the bird's wing surface.

Seen closer up, the out-thrust head and trailing legs make it clear that these are cranes, not geese or herons. Geese don't trail their legs, and herons don't fly with straight necks. The wings of a sandhill are more rounded on the ends than those of geese, the primaries clutching the air like outspread human fingers. Migrating cranes will sometimes pull a leg up into their bodies for warmth, though that inefficient posture is not maintained for long. A flying sandhill seems determined to reach a distant objective, its legs dangling idly as if the bird had concluded, "I won't need *these* for a while."

The distinctive wing beat pattern also distinguishes sandhills from such birds as geese. Sandhills sweep their wings slowly on the downstroke, bringing them up sharply. The more alarmed the birds are, the quicker the upstroke, though the downstroke doesn't seem to vary. Small subspecies flap faster, generating 10 to 20 percent more wing beats per minute than greater sandhills.

Although they usually take several running steps before launching themselves into the air, the sandhills make flying look easy once they're aloft. The birds have been clocked at speeds of 25 to 38 miles an hour. Sandhill flocks often appear to be playing in the air. The cranes sideslip, crisscross, and swap positions, apparently reveling in the sheer fun of flying.

Upon landing, sandhills often run a step or two while backstroking. At other times, they bounce several feet off the ground. The difference probably relates to the amount of headwind the crane lands in. The transition from flying to walking sometimes seems a bit awkward. Dayton Hyde, the nature

---

Upper left: The sandhill's red crown is a patch of naked skin that starts at the base of the bill.
Lower left: What appears to be the crane's tail is actually an extension of the wing feathers.

writer who raised several sandhills on his Oregon ranch, notes: "There is in a sandhill crane no movement, no action not of immaculate grace, unless it is at the moment they first touch land from flight. But then, once settled, they are pure grace again with elegant and measured step, as though that one ungainly moment had never been."

THE MIGRATING SANDHILL

A bird that migrates has struck a bargain with the universe. By shifting locales, the migrator can select for itself a region offering favorable weather and abundant food. In case there is a local food shortage, drought, or other adversity, the fiddlefooted migrator can open its wings and exercise its prerogative to go wherever it chooses.

Of course, there are penalties. Some lesser and Canadian sandhills spend four months of each year in migration. Migrating is exhausting and inherently hazardous. The birds spend much time on unfamiliar terrain, where they are vulnerable to accidents. When you are a young crane with a broken wing, you don't go to the hospital. You die. Among sandhill populations that migrate, more than half of all deaths occur during migration. Crane biologists note that the main "predator" of sandhill cranes on the Platte is the power line.

Migrators also have to accept a rigid schedule. This is particularly demanding for lesser sandhills, the birds with the longest biannual journey and the shortest nesting season. Some lessers migrate over 7,000 miles a year. Since they don't have the luxury of waiting for ideal travel conditions, these cranes often have to punch a path through heavy weather. When they alight on the breeding grounds, lesser sandhills have precious little time in which to bring off their broods.

Sandhill cranes apparently have a number of means for navigating when migrating. Whenever possible, they choose to fly in clear or mostly clear weather. Sandhills definitely prefer to migrate with sunlight or moonlight illuminating landmarks that aid their navigation.

Yet it isn't that simple. In research programs, cranes have shown a remarkable facility for finding their way around. Young cranes kept for a time at a refuge in Texas were taken away in an enclosed truck. They later returned to the refuge, having somehow discovered the way back, although they could not have done so in the usual way.

Any large-bodied bird that migrates long distances must fly with maximum energy efficiency. Sandhills minimize their energy expenditure by taking advantage of tail winds, by flying in formation, and by soaring.

A soaring crane rides the air with motionless wings like a turkey buzzard.

Upper left: Cranes launching from water. Lower left: Aloft! A sandhill in mid-air, legs dangling idly.

Overall Breeding and Migration Routes of the Sandhill Crane

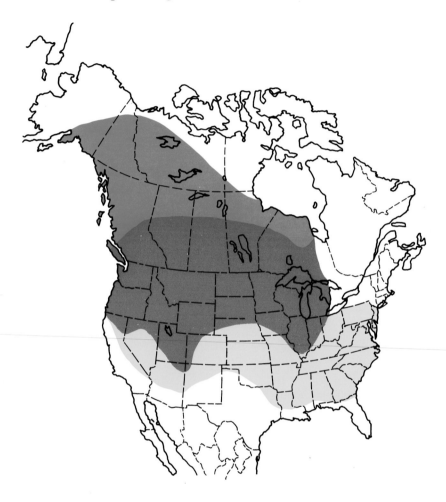

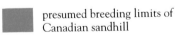 presumed breeding limits of
Canadian sandhill

 presumed breeding limits of
greater sandhill

northern wintering limits of all
sandhill species

Based on a map that appeared in Paul A. Johnsgard's Cranes of the World
(Indiana University Press, 1983).

Rising columns of warm air called thermals keep soaring cranes aloft. Some areas of the landscape, such as plowed fields, absorb more solar heat than adjacent marshes. The resulting heat differential can set up a thermal. Soaring requires only 30 percent of the energy needed for flapping flight. Sandhills do much of their migrating from mid-morning to afternoon, when thermals are strongest.

A migrating flock of sandhills announces itself long before it's seen. The trilling *gar-ooo-a-a, gar-ooo-a-a* can be heard from as far as three miles away. Spotting the source of the music usually requires minutes of scrutiny, because the flock will often be a faint, sketchy formation flying so high that the heads and legs are invisible to the naked eye. Sandhills have been spotted flying four miles high, and they typically migrate a mile above earth.

Migrating cranes might arrange themselves in V's, long lines, X's, or other shapes. Though they sometimes break into disorganized smaller groups when soaring, sandhills usually take advantage of the draft effect, with the lead bird carving a path in the wind for those behind.

Soaring sandhills are a stirring sight as they wheel gracefully on a thermal, each motionless bird embracing the air with extended wings like an elegant kite. Corkscrewing its way from one horizon to another, the flock hitchhikes from thermal to thermal across the sky.

WALKING, RUNNING, SWIMMING

A walking crane jerks its head with each step, as if to counterbalance a weight shift. The faster it walks, the more pronounced that action becomes.

A crane's long, naked legs are well-adapted for walking in water and mucky soil. As cranes pull their feet up, their toes clench, making it easier to withdraw a foot from a sloppy marsh bottom.

Some cranes, especially juveniles, throw their wings open when running, using the resistance of the wind as a sort of mobile cane to steady themselves. Sandhills run with a bouncy, trotting action. They're surprisingly fast. Researchers have attempted to run away from sandhill colts, but the birds effortlessly outpaced the ponderous humans.

Sandhill crane chicks can swim, and are quite buoyant and comfortable in the water. The buoyancy is useful, for many greater sandhills nest in marshes, with the nest protected from predators by a moat of water.

FEEDING AND DRINKING

Sandhills are omnivores. The term refers to animals that eat both vegetable and animal foods, but in the case of sandhills it means they eat just about *anything*. Their flexible, opportunistic diet is surely one of the reasons these cranes have survived for so many centuries. Evolution has generally dealt harshly with picky eaters.

Sandhills consume aquatic invertebrates, insects of all sorts, earthworms, snakes, frogs and other amphibians, small mammals, young birds, bird eggs, seeds, grass shoots, grain, tubers, berries, lichen, and the leaves of some aquatic plants. Oddly enough, although they resemble fish-eating birds right down to the sharp bill, the cranes rarely eat fish. Sandhills are primarily vegetarians, supplementing plant food with about ten percent animal matter.

Sandhill diets vary enormously by season. The birds take advantage of the most seasonally abundant foods. For example, migrating cranes eat a great deal of corn, wheat, and milo. Cranes in spring make a special effort to consume animal matter; they expend more energy than they acquire doing this, but something motivates the birds to

Left: The crane clenches its toes as it pulls its feet up, making walking easier in sloppy marshes.
Above: Sandhills often thrash their food around in water before eating it.

eat foods that supply nutrients important for egg and embryo formation. Sandhills sometimes switch diets for no apparent reason, suddenly rejecting a food they had eagerly consumed a day earlier. The obvious explanation is that the birds become bored with too much of the same fare, just as we do.

Chicks thrive on and require high protein animal food. They primarily feed upon earthworms, beetles, spiders, and other abundant insects. A young sandhill that was raised by Lawrence Walkinshaw would eat 200 worms in a morning and then gulp down an equal number in the afternoon. When grasshoppers become abundant, they're consumed in equal numbers. The colts of migrating sandhills begin eating grain just in time to benefit from its availability during the southward migration.

Walkinshaw tells the story of a tame Florida sandhill that loved horseflies. Each day during horsefly season, the crane walked to six neighboring homes. The bird chirped politely at the door, requesting admission. Inside, it then walked about the house, picking all the horseflies off the screen doors and windows before moving on to the next home. That crane also knew enough to avoid homes where its unique pest control service was not welcome.

Dayton Hyde was impressed by the ability of cranes to hold pests in check. Two cranes eradicated the grasshoppers from a heavily infested four-acre patch. During an outbreak of meadow mice that decimated crops on nearby ranches, Hyde's sandhills (with a little help from coyotes) kept his mouse population harmlessly low. A sandhill hearing a mouse or mole burrowing underground will cock its head sideways to fix the location, then stab with deadly precision. The animal is usually killed with a puncture wound just behind the head.

The bill of a sandhill is a powerful and versatile device. The bird uses its bill like a garden tool to dig and probe for insects, frequently feeding three to five inches below the surface.

A sandhill cannot swallow large food items. The crane will thrash or stab a large morsel until it is bite-sized. The bird holds a piece of food, then snaps its head forward and back to toss the item toward its throat, perhaps throwing and catching the food twice before swallowing. A sandhill tastes food items before swallowing them. If water is available, the bird will often thrash the food around in the liquid before eating it.

Sandhills are exceptionally deft with their bills. A recent visitor to the International Crane Foundation knelt near a sandhill colt. Spotting her shiny hearing aid, the crane plucked it from the visitor's ear without hurting its owner. Dayton Hyde considered one of his male sandhills so gentle that he

A sandhill attempts to devour a tasty ribbon snake.

would have "trusted him with his great surgeon's beak to pick a hay seed from my eye."

Cranes acquire water with their food, but frequently need to drink it directly. A sandhill eating animal food doesn't need to drink nearly as often as a crane consuming grain. The nostrils of a sandhill are placed high, permitting the bird to scoop water while keeping nasal passages dry. The crane drops its bill, scoops a load of water, then lifts its head to send the water sloshing down its throat.

THE SANDHILL ON DEFENSE

The sandhill's reproductive strategy puts a high premium on the adults' ability to protect their colts. Because cranes are large enough to warrant a concerted stalk from a predator, especially when nesting, the cranes must be able to mount a formidable defense.

A sandhill has three weapons, and apparently chooses among them by judging how severe the threat appears to be. The wings can deliver powerful blows. The toes have sharp claws—razor-sharp, according to those who have learned the hard way. The dagger-like bill strikes with uncanny accuracy at distances of up to four feet. People who handle cranes in research and management programs wear armor of stout leather and canvas, plus high-impact glasses to protect their eyes.

A sandhill defending its young is an imposing sight. The crane, already four to five feet tall, spreads its wings and flares its feathers to appear larger. Sandhills have chased away coyotes, dogs, caribou, and moose. (A sandhill chasing a moose is giving away a weight advantage of about 1,800 pounds!) Sandhills have killed hunting dogs while defending their young.

The most famous encounter between a human and a sandhill featured artist and naturalist John James Audubon. Audubon shot the bird along the Missouri River, wounding it. When he pursued it on foot, the crane turned on him and ". . . raised itself to the full stretch of its body, legs, and neck, ruffled its feathers, shook them, and advanced toward me with open bill, and eyes glancing with anger." Audubon quickly learned that he couldn't outrun a crane. The bird chased him into the river, and pressed the charge until Audubon was up to his neck. Sandhills are not normally aggressive, but they defend themselves ably.

LIFE SPAN

Sandhills probably have a potential life of 20 to 30 years. There isn't a great deal of information on the longevity of cranes, but enough to suggest that the upper-end capacity of a bird in captivity can be high. One Siberian crane lived to 82 years, for example, and other species have topped 40 years. The record for a sandhill in captivity seems to be 24 years.

The life span of sandhills in the wild is much shorter. Information from banding data is confusing, because hunting mortality is such a large factor and because the age of many banded birds is not known. A great many sandhills die within their first year or two, but those surviving that perilous period have a good chance to live longer, some as long as 15 years.

DANCING

Sandhills were called "preacher birds" by early settlers, because the antics of the birds resembled a preacher leading his congregation. (Preachers were apparently more entertaining once than most are now.) This joyous "dancing" is one of the most remarkable and thrilling sights in the animal world.

Dancing cranes bow ceremoniously to each other, bounce into the air as high as 20 feet, hop about, flap their

The crane's toes have razor-sharp claws, according to handlers who have learned the hard way.

wings, throw back their heads, pirouette, toss sticks into the air, stand on one foot and then the other, drop a single wing in a studied gesture, or jump about with stiff legs.

Biologists have changed in their thinking about why sandhills dance. Dancing was once considered a mating ritual, practiced mainly on the breeding grounds. But sandhills mate for life, so there is no great need for courtship. And while dancing is more prevalent in spring, cranes dance at all times of year. Moreover, dancing is not limited to mated pairs. Juveniles and other unmated sandhills dance, as do groups of several sandhills. Chicks dance when they're just two days old.

The most recent research suggests that dancing is primarily a courtship ritual for unpaired birds. Paired adults dance very little on the breeding grounds, whereas dancing is prominent among unpaired birds during the weeks preceding the nesting season.

Beyond that, cranes often dance when they are obviously frustrated or excited, so dancing seems a release of pent-up energy, or a "displacement" behavior. This is evidenced by the fact that no sandhills dance as often as two- and three-year old captive sandhills. Dancing generally thwarts aggression, and it could fulfill other social functions not yet understood.

THE SANDHILL'S REPRODUCTIVE STRATEGY

There are two basic strategies by which bird populations maintain their numbers. Some species can accept heavy annual losses because they reproduce at such high rates. Other species are far less prolific, yet maintain their numbers by minimizing mortality. The bobwhite quail has poor prospects for a long life, but its reproductive program allows it to outproduce its losses. Sandhill cranes represent the other extreme.

Each strategy has its advantages and disadvantages. The high-mortality, high-productivity birds can be hurt badly by adverse weather when nesting. A bad spring, with cold weather and too much rain, is bad news for quail. On the other hand, a quail population can quickly expand to take advantage of good times. Roller-coaster population fluctuations are typical of birds that raise big clutches to make up for heavy annual losses.

To reduce mortality, sandhills form secure family bonds, raise their young with tender devotion, and defend the chicks vigorously. There are costs. Being good parents requires the expenditure of time and energy. Sandhills also "waste" time reinforcing social bonds. The sandhills' anxiety about predation sometimes seems out of proportion to any real threat. It seems that

A sandhill dances in a Nebraska cornfield.

eternal vigilance is not only the price of liberty, it is the price of low productivity for a sandhill.

Since they live longer than many birds, sandhills would quickly overpopulate their habitat were they to raise large broods. As we've seen, they do not. About 20 percent of the nests failed altogether in one study. At most, a pair can hope to bring two chicks south.

Other factors depress sandhill fertility. A sandhill doesn't reach sexual maturity until it's two or three years of age, further limiting reproductive potential. And if the birds are disturbed while nesting, they are less likely to re-nest than many bird species.

It all adds up to low reproductive potential. The annual increase in the population, called the "recruitment rate" by biologists, is only 9 to 11 percent for sandhills. That's quite low.

Under normal conditions, population levels for birds with low reproductive potential are very stable. But conditions have not been normal for the sandhills since European settlers began rearranging the face of the North American continent. Human predation and human economic activities have hurt most animal populations, to be sure, but they represent a special threat to a bird like a crane.

In the case of some species, humans can behave irresponsibly and later undo the damage with the aid of the birds' potent reproductive powers. But where birds like the sandhill are concerned, ecological mistakes might have lasting effects that require a great deal of money and effort to undo, if indeed they can be undone. No more tragic example could exist than the sandhill's cousin, North America's exceedingly endangered whooping crane.

Human activities pose a special threat to families like this one.

THE YEAR OF THE SANDHILL

SANDHILL SPRING

After wintering in northern Mexico, western Texas, and eastern New Mexico, the lesser and Canadian sandhill cranes often complete the 600-mile trip to the Platte River in one non-stop flight of 12 hours. With the assistance of southerly winds, the cranes may average 50 miles an hour. The birds usually arrive along the Platte in early February, and February being what it is in the Midwest, the cranes frequently have to contend with snowstorms and swirling winds.

The great grey birds are a welcome sight to winter-weary Nebraskans. They stay for about six weeks, storing up body reserves while they wait for advancing spring warmth to unlock their frozen breeding grounds.

While the sandhills work on storing fat and the nutrients needed to form eggs and embryos, they prepare for the breeding season. Above all, spring is the time for dancing, and much of the pair-formation dancing takes place in the wet pastures along the Platte, the ancestral feeding grounds where cranes danced for centuries before humans began planting row crops nearby.

One day in early April, when the winds are favorable, the mid-continental sandhills mount the skies and move farther north. They don't leave *en masse*, but their departure is abrupt. Naturalist Walter Breckenridge, writing in 1945, described a departure:

Breeding, Distribution, and Wintering Areas

lesser sandhill breeding range		residential distributions of Florida and Mississippi sandhill
Canadian sandhill breeding range		major wintering areas of migratory sandhills
greater sandhill breeding range		staging areas of migratory sandhills

Based on a map that appeared in Paul A. Johnsgard's Cranes of the World
(Indiana University Press, 1983).

Gradually the clamoring mass of birds rose higher and higher toward the massive white cumulus clouds floating in the deep blue sky. And as they rose they slowly began to organize themselves into a huge circling whirlpool-like formation that turned ever so slowly and all the while towering higher and higher. Their calls gradually became less and less distinct and their huge forms smaller and smaller until finally the highest bird had to be followed with 8X binoculars.

The migrating flocks travel only by day unless bright moonlight aids navigation, in which case they cruise the night skies for a while before landing to rest. Migrating lesser sandhills average 50 to 70 miles a day in a series of short hops after leaving the Platte. They do not stage in great concentrations again.

Meanwhile, other populations of sandhills are on the move. The Great Lakes greater sandhills leave Florida in February and head toward the Jasper-Pulaski Fish and Wildlife area in northwestern Indiana. These birds do not stage in massive numbers in spring as the smaller races do, and they might not even stop at Jasper-Pulaski. But their physical needs are the same, and they generally tarry in the Midwest for a time, feeding on waste corn. Peak

Cranes may fly at night if bright moonlight is present to aid navigation.

numbers come in mid-March, when 2,000 to 3,000 cranes roost in the marshes of Jasper-Pulaski and forage in the area.

These birds are moving north again by the middle of April. They arrive at their breeding grounds in the Great Lakes states—primarily Michigan, Wisconsin, and Minnesota—in April.

Similar movements at about the same time are made by the Rocky Mountain and California flocks of greaters.

While the largest race of sandhills is in its nesting areas by the middle of April, the lessers and Canadians push north for another whole month before reaching their destination on the coast of Alaska. The arctic-nesting cranes can't afford to waste time, for in about two months their young must be able to fly all the way south again, just ahead of wintry blasts.

NESTING

The three basic nesting habitat requirements of sandhills are: large areas of shallow water; isolation from human activity; and dry uplands nearby with a good supply of food. Nesting sandhills seek out desolate, flat, open areas where they can spot predators at great distances.

Shortly after arriving in their nesting areas, the adults drive away last year's young. These youngsters move off to form "bachelor" flocks. They might get together with their parents again when the new young are able to fly, but they might not. One function of the family breakup is to promote mixing that ensures genetic variation. The only truly durable social unit among sandhills is the mated pair and the young it currently tends. Larger flocks are just loose aggregations of families.

On the nesting grounds, mated pairs perform an important display known as the unison call. The male and female stand together to declare their territorial claim in a series of clarion, antiphonal calls. The gender-related behavior during this ritual provides the only sure means of identifying the sex of each crane within a pair. The male tosses his head to a vertical position with each call. The female cries twice for each call of the male, and her voice is distinctly shriller. She begins with her head held level and tosses it upward only about 45 degrees while calling. This strident, percussive call is only performed by mated pairs.

Sandhills defend their nesting areas against other sandhills with determination. Their aggression is remarkable, for sandhills are gregarious birds at all times except when nesting. Mated pairs return to the same regions each year to nest, although they rarely build nests on the same spot. With birds that mate for life, returning to the same breeding grounds has survival advantages. The

Sandhill nests have been described as "soggy haystacks."

birds fare better when they are nesting on familiar territory.

If another sandhill trespasses on a pair's territory, the male drives off the intruder with a head-down display of his enlarged, enflamed crown patch. The male's vigilance is important. If he's lost to a predator or an accident, the female will probably forfeit her territory.

This territorial aggression, so unlike sandhill behavior at all other times of the year, serves several functions. Territorial aggression reduces predation and distributes nesting pairs evenly over the best habitat. When nests are too close together because too many birds are nesting in the same habitat, males spend too much time defending boundaries. Then, because the males aren't available to tend the nest when the female is forced to leave, predators slip in and pilfer the eggs.

The average territory defended by an adult pair is 400 acres, but there is considerable variation. Researchers have seen sandhills defend as many as 1,000 or as few as 42 acres. Several factors might account for that difference. Most important among them is the richness of the food supply on uplands adjacent to the nest. Cranes can afford to nest in

The eggs in an untended nest are vulnerable to predators.

higher densities (defending smaller territories) when food is abundant.

Choosing a high-quality habitat is crucial to the success of the nesting pair's efforts. The territory must contain a considerable amount of food, since it has to support two adult cranes and one or two voracious chicks. Later, when the young have "fledged" (gained the ability to fly), the cranes can relocate to habitat that offers more food or greater security. But for the first weeks of life, the pair's chosen territory must supply *everything*—food, security, and fresh water.

Sandhill nests aren't pretty or fancy.

The cranes make them by rooting up dead vegetation, raking it inward with their bills. The best definition of the materials used is: Whatever's there suffices. Cattails, sedges, sticks, grasses, mosses, and other materials are piled up in a mound. Nest size varies, depending on how much suitable material happens to be nearby. The end result has been described as a soggy haystack with a central oval depression.

Security is utmost in the minds of the birds. The nests of lesser sandhills are protected by the empty land around them, but greater sandhills often build raised nests in shallow water for even

Fortunately, parents like this nesting Florida sandhill defend the nest with great determination.

greater safety. All the nests in one Michigan study of greater sandhills were surrounded by water and sheltered from humans. During nesting, sandhills are so profoundly disturbed by human interference that the birds are likely to abandon the nest if a researcher examines it in order to count the eggs.

Recent research suggests that dancing is not important to mated pairs at this time of year, though unison calling is. Some researchers think the male is most intimately tuned in to the surroundings. His gonadal and hormonal development are triggered by signals coming from the environment. He probably responds most to day-length, and immediate weather factors have a secondary influence. Through unison calling, the male encourages his mate to be ready to mate when he is, and when the time is right.

As part of the nesting process, adult sandhills paint themselves with silt containing ferrous oxides. They pick up the rusty silt on their bills and spread it over their feathers. The birds that were dun grey in April become a lovely sedge color when nesting. The acquired color, reminiscent of the red coats of summer whitetails, perfectly matches the tawny vegetation where cranes nest. In the whole world of birds, only one other bird (another crane, the Eurasian) paints itself in cryptic colors.

Biologists have been reluctant to admit that this is intentional behavior, yet surely it is. The iron-rich muds are not accidentally acquired while feeding, as once thought, but smeared on

Left: Success! Escaping the egg can be an entire day's work for a sandhill chick. Above: During the nesting period, cranes cover their feathers with rusty silt.

with persistent effort to all areas of the sandhill's body that can be reached by a muddy bill. It's surely no accident that cranes paint themselves exactly the color that is most prevalent in their surroundings. Nor can it be a coincidence that the painted adults exactly match the color of newly hatched chicks. A sandhill with a bright green leg tag was observed painting the *tag* with rusty silt, further evidence that the camouflage treatment is intentional. Later, the oxide-stained plumage is lost in the summer moult.

Because of their varying life circumstances, sandhills of different subtypes lay eggs at different times. Some Florida and Mississippi sandhills produce eggs in March. Lessers breeding in Alaska mainly produce in June.

THE YOUNG

Sandhills usually lay two eggs, but sometimes one is laid and, rarely, three are produced. The eggs are laid two to three days apart. They are buff or olive, with brown or lilac spots. Incubation begins when the first egg is laid, which is not a universal practice among birds. Both adults incubate the eggs, each being equipped with two naked brood patches along the sternum for keeping the eggs warm.

The adults take turns on the nest, switching places about four times a day. Both adults might leave the nest to feed in the warmth of midday when the eggs will not be threatened by chilly air. They won't be far away, though, and they'll keep a sharp eye on the nest all the while. Depending on where they brood, sandhills might defend nests against glaucous gulls, jaegers, raccoons, or coyotes. Humans take some eggs as well.

Incubation takes 28 to 31 days. When its time has come, the chick entombed in the first-laid egg will pip a lateral crack in the shell and push the end off. The effort of escaping the egg can take a whole day. Finally, the chick tumbles into the outside world, soggy and panting, the victor in the first test of its ability to survive.

The chick is soon dry, fluffy, and cute, although it looks as though it was shipped into the world with a set of legs intended for a larger bird. Chicks are a tawny sedge color with light eye rings. The mother often offers pieces of the eggshell to the youngster as food. Chicks spend their first hours huddling under the mother or crawling up on her back.

The chick tries to stand and walk within hours of being born. Soon the first-born joins its father in nearby grasslands, to be fed and taught how to find food on its own. The female continues to brood the second egg.

Young birds are born without the ability to regulate their own body temperatures. Acquiring that ability, called

reaching the point of endothermy, occurs much more quickly among the lesser sandhills of the arctic than among the Florida sandhills.

SANDHILL SIBLINGS

As a result of the "asynchronous" incubation pattern, the first chick hatches a day or two before the second chick. What follows from that pattern is troublesome to many sandhill fans.

Shortly after the second chick has gained the ability to walk and the whole family comes together, the siblings begin charging at each other like mortal enemies. They peck and fight. Fights are particularly vicious at feeding times during the first two or three weeks of life.

Ultimately, the more vigorous chick—usually the older and significantly stronger one—will bully the weaker chick until it loses the will to fight. It then runs off and perishes. Dayton Hyde attempted to retrieve the runaway chicks of his pet sandhills, but found they were suicidally determined to run away again, even at the cost of leaving their mothers.

This does not *always* happen. The first-born chick stays mainly with the male, and the second stays mainly with the female. While the siblings sleep together under their mother at night, they do not see each other and do not fight. If the parents succeed in keeping the young apart enough of the time during the first weeks of life, both chicks can survive. Aggression between chicks subsides after about 50 days. More often than not, however, sibling rivalry reduces the family of four sandhills to three. Less than one family in five brings two chicks south to the wintering grounds.

The "fratricide" is hard to accept because the sacrificed chick seems genetically qualified to survive. Humans, who tend to be jolted by all the mortality they observe in wildlife populations, take comfort from the notion that animals die because they are old, sick, or genetically unfit. But that consoling rationale does not apply here. To routinely sacrifice the second-born chick for no apparent reason seems wasteful, even cruel. Why couldn't both chicks survive?

There are several answers. Having a second chick is a sensible security measure for sandhills in case the first-born falls to a predator or an accident. Sometimes the second chick is more vigorous than the first, in which case fratricide benefits the species by promoting the most viable chick. Further, cranes are long-lived birds that do not need to raise two chicks each season; indeed, they would overpopulate their habitat if they could routinely fledge two chicks.

Raising chicks to fledging is difficult, demanding work. When whooping crane nests are robbed of one egg, *more* chicks survive to fledging than would have survived if the nests not been tampered with. Two parents are more effective when caring for one chick than they are when they divide their attention between two. So, when a sandhill family drops from four to three, the "loss" is often a gain, for it improves the chances that the dominant chick will survive.

The best explanation for the fratricidal enigma is the way it matches family size with food availability. When food is plentiful in a pair's territory, each adult can tend and feed a chick. When food is harder to secure, the efforts of two adults are needed to feed a single chick. The sandhill's reproductive program maximizes the chances that the most vigorous chick will survive, while allowing for the possibility that the pair will fledge a bonus chick.

Sandhills don't always succeed in bringing up even one chick. Dayton Hyde writes that it's easy to judge the family status of feeding cranes. Adults feeding apart probably have a chick apiece. Adults feeding together are tending a single offspring. But if all of the chicks have been lost, he writes, "There is a desultory, forlorn manner about them, an aimless method of feeding, and their concern at the approach of danger is only for themselves. In sorrow, they fly silently away without trying to protest or decoy."

GROWING LIKE TOPSY

The early development of sandhill chicks is astonishing. They walk within a day of being born and are able to swim vigorously within two or three days. A sandhill chick gains in body weight by about ten percent per day. The greatest amount of weight gain happens between the second and seventh weeks of life.

Growth rates vary with different subtypes. Lesser sandhill chicks born in late May will be almost as tall as their parents by August. In only eight weeks, a tiny lesser sandhill chick must become a six-pound crane with the strength to fly almost 4,000 miles. Long arctic days and a wealth of insects make that miracle possible. The chicks of greater sandhills develop a little more slowly, beginning to fly ten weeks after hatching.

Entomologist Joel Welty has pointed out major differences in the development of two seemingly similar birds. Sandhill chicks are "nidifugous" (nest-fleeing) birds. As such, they have no early need for strong wings, but must be able to walk and run almost at once. Their wings develop relatively slowly, while their legs develop quickly. The most rapid leg development comes in their second week, and it's essentially complete at 32 days. A crane chick can run when just two days old.

The stork, a bird with similar body

architecture, develops the other way around. The chicks of "altricial" birds like storks are helpless outside the nest. Since stork chicks are brooded in nests above the ground, their first developmental need is wings. Strong legs, in fact, would be a hazard. Baby storks are blind and helpless at an age when sandhills are scooting around in the upland grass with their parents. At 29 days, a stork's wings and feathers are close to maturity, yet its legs are weak and undeveloped until about the 38th day of life.

The sandhill family feeds in the uplands, often returning to the marsh at night to sleep on the nest or on sleeping mounds built by the adults. Daily, adults lead the colts into the fields, offering them food and demonstrating how the colts can find their own. Soon the lessons include preflight "ground training," learning to run with outstretched wings.

Before long, the colts take to the air. When that happens, the crane family moves to fields rich with food. There, they might join other sandhills in loose flocks, ending the only period when sandhills don't choose to be close to others of their species. Late summer is spent foraging and strengthening the colts' flying muscles.

The adults go through their annual moult at about this time. Intriguingly, some sandhills moult in stages, while others moult all at once. The difference is related to the security of their surroundings. The greater sandhills that nest around the Great Lakes or the Rocky Mountains moult a little at a time, never losing the ability to fly. The lessers in the relatively predator-free tundra pass through a sudden moult.

SOUTH AGAIN

It isn't cold weather but a shortage of food that sends the cranes flying south again. Sandhills are tough birds, well adapted to withstand cold weather. But they must eat; indeed, they must eat a great deal to maintain growth in the colts and to fuel the muscles that carry them nearly the length of the continent. The approach of cold weather shuts down insect life and other food sources, forcing the birds to relocate.

The cranes begin making more and more practice flights, and one day an older crane will lead the spiraling flock off toward the wintering grounds. Undertaking a series of short hops, the arctic-nesting sandhills move south and east. While crossing the rugged mountains of the Alaskan Range, the cranes might be as high as 20,000 feet above sea level. They pick up fellow travelers as they go.

Food becomes suddenly abundant when the cranes reach the wheat fields of Saskatchewan. There, some birds stage to prepare for the rest of their

A solitary feather signifies the crane's moulting season.

journey, although others trickle south to fatten on grain in North Dakota, Idaho, and other states in the Central Flyway. Within these northern states, cranes can find many arid, lightly populated regions where marshes provide security and isolation from humans.

The farmers who feed these fall cranes rarely do so willingly. Sandhills eat a lot of grain, and they trample a great deal more. By defecating, cranes reduce the market value of still more grain. Because sandhills forage on farms in sparsely settled areas where soils are poor, crane predation can spell the difference between profit and loss to some farmers.

Irritated landowners sometimes shoot cranes to protect their crops. Hunting seasons were instituted mainly to reduce these illegal shootings. Apart from hunting, the two greatest sources of mortality for adult cranes are flying accidents (primarily striking power lines) and poaching (primarily by enraged farmers).

The Great Lakes and Rocky Mountain sandhills don't need to move as early as the lessers and Canadians. But by October, flocks of these majestic cranes are in the air.

The Great Lakes cranes stage at Jasper-Pulaski each fall, arriving in September and peaking at numbers of 10,000 to 14,000 birds in late October.

This is the largest concentration of greater sandhills, and it draws crowds of crane admirers. Many of these people recall a time when Great Lakes sandhill numbers were sadly depleted. In 1942, the staging peak at Jasper-Pulaski was only 160 cranes. The sandhills roost in shallow marsh, feeding primarily on corn in "lure crops" planted for them by the Indiana Department of Natural Resources.

Some sandhills reach their wintering grounds as early as September, but that is unusual. By late November, the California, Rocky Mountain, and Great Lakes flocks have settled into wintering areas, primarily marshy refuges in the Southwest.

Last to arrive are the arctic-nesting birds. Many of them finally spin out of the sky to drop into refuges in the Staked Plains of eastern New Mexico and northwestern Texas. The alkaline water here is unfit for human consumption, and the land is so featureless that Spanish explorers feared getting lost if they didn't periodically drive stakes in the ground as reference points. It's a place with a big sky and nothing much to break up the view—a place where cranes can see danger coming from a long ways off. It's just the sort of place that makes humans feel uncomfortable and sandhills feel at home.

SANDHILL SOCIETY

SANDHILL INTERACTIONS

Animals that lead solitary lives have little need to coordinate their activities with others of their kind. A few devices to mark a territory, a few courtship gestures used once a year—that's as much social "language" as they need.

Things could not be more different for the highly social sandhill crane. Dayton Hyde writes, "There is nothing more pathetically lonely than a single sandhill crane, for by the very essence of their nature they are gregarious." Except when nesting, a sandhill wants to be with other sandhills, particularly its own family. Crane family members not able to see each other endeavor to maintain voice contact at all times.

Such a bird needs something like language to control and organize social interactions. To use a simple example, sandhills need some sort of air traffic control system. The solitary egret wading through a marsh can take to its wings whenever it chooses, but the sandhill surrounded by others must be more orderly. It must announce its intention to take off with voice and body gestures before committing to flight.

Social interactions among sandhills are mediated by at least three devices. The birds are marked in ways that inform other sandhills of their social status; they communicate with each other through calls that have specific meanings; and they interact by means of stylized acts that biologists call "behaviors."

Crane calls have little in common with bird songs. Many perching birds engage in extended, complex, and variable vocalizations. Crane calls are short, are not subject to individual variation, and are innate rather than learned. For example, the unison call is the unison call, no matter which sandhills do it. There is one right way to call, and it will always be understood in the same way by other sandhills. Since each crane call has a specific meaning, it can be part of a universal auditory vocabulary.

Similarly, there is a visual vocabulary based on a fixed repertoire of behaviors. A casual observer watching cranes interacting would not understand that what seem to be spontaneous, flexible responses are often stereotyped behaviors. But the cranes understand, which is what counts.

Now researchers understand, and that counts, too. Careful observation of sandhills has allowed researchers to recognize calls and set behaviors. Study has also revealed the usual context and significance of the calls and behaviors. In other words, human observers have cracked much of the code for sandhill discourse. This breakthrough has in turn yielded many insights concerning the sandhill's social structure.

A full analysis of sandhill calls and behaviors is much too complex for a book like this, but it will be useful to present a few examples from the research of Karen Voss, Thomas Tacha, and George Archibald.

THE AMAZING TRACHEA

Nothing about the sandhill anatomy is as remarkable as its windpipe, or trachea. The trachea is a long, flexible tube that runs between the throat and chest. Tough, cartilaginous rings keep the trachea from collapsing or binding. There's nothing strange about that. But while a typical adult sandhill might have a neck 23 inches long, its trachea is about 48 inches.

The first obvious question is: Where are those extra 25 inches? They're located in the chest area, lying in convoluted loops along the sternum under the wing muscles. While the calls of cranes are often described as "bugling" or "trumpeting," the sandhill's windpipe has more in common with the French horn, a musical instrument that conveys a sort of moody beauty similar to the effect of crane calls.

A young crane is not born with a coiled trachea. As the crane develops, the trachea grows much faster than the rest of the body. Soon enough, all that extra trachea has to go somewhere, so it coils along the sternum.

The next obvious question is: Why? Why does a bird with two feet of neck have a trachea as long as a vacuum

It's a long neck, but an even longer trachea.

cleaner hose? The answer isn't simple.

There are some obvious drawbacks to having such an extravagant trachea. A long trachea weighs more than a normal one, takes up space in the chest, and has more wind resistance (which would increase the effort needed to breathe). If true, this is odd. One would hardly expect a migrating bird to be burdened with an inefficient breathing tube.

Observers have pointed out that a human would die of asphyxiation if forced to breathe through a windpipe that long. Our lungs could never clear the stale air out of such a tube. But the comparison is misleading. Instead of lungs like ours, the birds have a number of air sacs that are much more efficient at transferring oxygen to the blood. Moreover, since the growing trachea increases in diameter as it lengthens, the bird suffers no great impediment to breathing as the trachea grows.

Still, when all factors are balanced out, anatomists conclude that sandhill tracheas (and those of other *Grus* cranes) are not as efficient as they could be. Again: Why? According to Paul Johnsgard, the University of Nebraska professor and authority on cranes, "It would . . . seem that the cranes have 'accepted' the respiratory penalties associated with an unusually long trachea (and thus an increased volume of 'dead' tracheal air to be exchanged with each breath) for certain acoustical benefits." In other words, crane tracheas don't function as efficiently as they might as breathing tubes, but do permit cranes to emit sounds that aren't possible with a short trachea.

Even that explanation is not easy to understand. In general, the cranes with the longest tracheas make the loudest, most penetrating calls. The whooping crane, with an even longer trachea than the sandhill, has a correspondingly booming voice. Yet the relationship is not simple. One study indicates that crane tracheas are much longer than they need be in order to create the frequencies emitted. The main advantage of extra-long tracheas might be the harmonics (overtones that are multiples of the base frequency) they make possible. Those harmonics enrich the vocalizations available to the cranes.

Crane music has always thrilled humans. Now research explains some of the basic physics underlying the mysterious qualities of crane calls. Clearly, being able to communicate by voice is extremely important to sandhills.

SANDHILL VOCALIZATIONS

Sandhill "speech" sounds like babble to humans, but several distinctive calls have been identified by Archibald. The following is a summary of the calls of *Grus* cranes, including the sandhill.

Young chicks make three calls. The

stress call indicates that the chicks are frightened, hungry, or unhappy about being separated from their parents. Chicks issue a plaintive food-begging call that disappears from their vocabulary at about 12 months of age, when they take charge of their own feeding.

One of the most interesting chick calls is also used by adults. The contact call is a purring noise that sounds surprisingly feline. Like cats, cranes purr when they seem contented. Cranes sometimes make this purring noise while sleeping.

When cranes begin to fly, they acquire a flight-intention call. And at about this age, cranes sometimes emit a rapid, high-pitched alarm call when confronted by something that frightens them.

When a colt with its parents feels threatened by other cranes or some other danger, it might use the guard call. This call is often acquired after the crane experiences its voice change, at a little less than one year old.

At about the same time, a young crane acquires a location call, a plaintive cry used to re-establish contact with family members after separation. It apparently works. Sandhills have a remarkable ability to find each other.

Voice communication is extremely important to sandhills.

In research studies, sandhill siblings that became separated were later able to locate each other among thousands of staging cranes.

Some calls are only used by adults, including a pre-copulation call and a nesting call. Most important of the adult calls, though, is the unison call. It strengthens pair bonds, advertises territory, and synchronizes the cranes' sexual development.

CHEEK MARKERS

Sandhill cheeks are either white, grey, or some smudgy mix of white and grey. The difference isn't aesthetic. According to Tacha, cheek color indicates the social status of a sandhill. Social status is determined not by any personal qualities possessed by a crane, but by age and family standing.

The age difference is important, as it tells other cranes whether a sandhill is sexually mature, and therefore a possible threat to pair bonds. Juveniles are identifiable to other cranes by the tawny feathers on their crowns and napes.

In terms of sandhill society, adult sandhills are classified as single, paired, or paired with juveniles. Mysteriously, parents and paired sandhills almost always have bright white cheeks. Unpaired sandhills have grey cheeks.

It's interesting that crane social standing is linked to being part of a family. In any aggressive encounter between adult cranes, the white-cheeked bird has higher status and will prevail. Presumably, this arrangement favors the cranes with the best chances of surviving—not the biggest or most aggressive cranes, but those enjoying the survival advantages of family membership. The connection between cheek color and family status serves to underline the implied logic of sandhill society: *Strong families are good for sandhills, individually and collectively.*

This does not explain why it's so important for a crane pair to know whether a third crane approaching them is paired or single. After all, if cranes "mate for life," an unattached crane should pose no threat to a pair bond. Why should cranes care about the marital status of other cranes?

The likeliest explanation arises from research on Florida sandhills, birds that are more easily studied since they stay put. Florida sandhills, according to research by Steve Nesbitt, *don't* simply mate for life. Once a pair forms a bond, mates, and produces young, "divorce" is extremely rare. But young cranes go through an experimental period during which they might have several "boyfriends" or "girlfriends" before "getting married." Thus, a young adult crane might become involved with four or five "significant others" before settling into a lasting relationship. Crane couples that mate but fail to produce

Married or single? Cheek coloring can give a crane's status away.

young are much more likely to divorce and form other pairings. So, in theory, crane pairings are somewhat vulnerable to intruders.

Though the sex of a sandhill is not advertised with obvious markings as is the case with such birds as pheasants, cranes can surely identify the sex of other cranes. The bills of the males are slightly longer relative to the rest of their heads, for example. There are behavioral differences, too. Males are more aggressive and domineering. Females are deferential and retain some of the infantile gestures of chicks (such as fluffing up) to indicate that they should not be subjected to aggressive attacks. When families are walking, the male always leads the female, which will be followed by the juvenile crane if there is one.

BEHAVIORS

Tacha and Voss have described and named a number of sandhill behaviors.

The tall alert is a behavior usually performed by the male of a family in response to a threat. The crane stands rigidly erect, with his neck stretched as high as it can go, looking straight ahead. This looks like a natural response to danger, but actually is a stylized behavior. The tall alert is quite contagious. When one bird does it, others copy.

The tall alert is highly associated with a particular threat—namely humans and their vehicles. Spring crane watchers often see the tall alert, because many of the birds have recently been hunted. A crane in the tall alert posture is indicating to other cranes that a human—a potentially dangerous predator—is uncomfortably close.

What humans call "dancing" in cranes is often a sequence of courtship behaviors strung together. One behavior is the bow. When bowing, a crane retracts its neck, lowers its head, bends down, and extends its wings. It then lunges upward before returning to the original position.

Stick-tossing behavior involves a similar body posture, but the crane seizes an object when its head is low and then explodes upward, flinging the object away before dropping to the retracted position again.

A series of bows and stick tosses, mixed with hops and leaps, is the basis for many sandhill dances. Dancing performs several social functions. The most important is forming pair bonds between cranes that have not yet made a firm commitment to a mate.

The flight intention behavior has been mentioned. A crane faces the wind, bends its neck, and holds its head forward. The actions are accompanied by the flight intention call.

In the attack behavior, a crane runs at its target and performs a karate-like

Sandhill Behaviors

Bowing

Stick-tossing

Raising tertials

Crouch/threat

Sandhill Behaviors

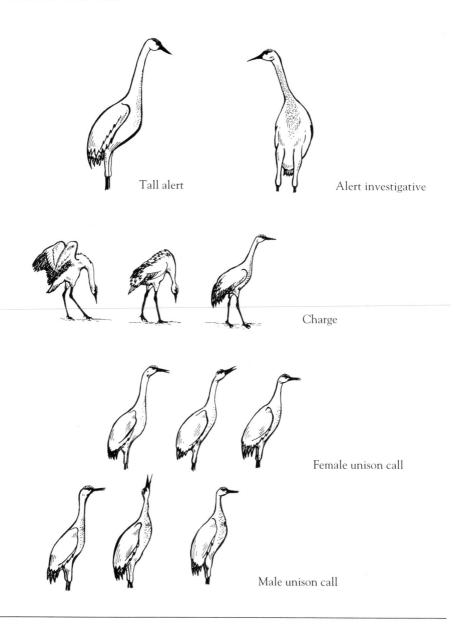

Tall alert

Alert investigative

Charge

Female unison call

Male unison call

jumping kick. Two cranes will do this until one retreats or signals submission. One signal of submission is the appeasement posture. In this behavior, the appeasing crane drops its body to the horizontal to look as low as possible, bending its neck to hold the head low but level.

In aggressive social interactions, a sandhill communicates threats with its red crown. This area of naked, papillose skin is connected to muscles, so the bird can enlarge or diminish the visible portion of the patch. The bird also controls the brightness of the skin. The size and color of the crown patch indicate how aroused or excited a sandhill is. A belligerent crane will hold its head downward, advertising its red crown to the target crane. A submissive crane carefully does not display its crown, nor will the crown be enflamed.

The charge is another of the crown-displaying behaviors. The crane walks forward with its head down very low, the crown exposed, and feathers raised at the base of the neck and back. The crane might jab at the ground. This behavior occurs in several contexts, including when a crane has just landed near a flock.

SANDHILL SOCIETY

In general, sandhill society conveys status and advantages to adult cranes

Sandhill Behaviors

Flight intention

Drinking

Attack sequence

that are paired and to juveniles under the care of parents. As in Dickensian England, orphans lead less privileged lives. Juvenile sandhills that still have parents experience fewer hostile contacts with other cranes and are able to spend twice as much time gleaning grain in winter as orphans.

Cracking the code of calls and behaviors is something like discovering the Rosetta stone of crane language.

With that knowledge, researchers can interpret crane discourse. For example, high levels of aggressive encounters in a particular setting might indicate that the sandhills are under unusual stress. Perhaps the birds' environment doesn't offer enough fresh water or roosting space. Wildlife managers will know what sorts of habitat improvements are required because, in effect, the cranes have told them!

Frequent aggressive encounters like this one may indicate that sandhills are experiencing unusual stress.

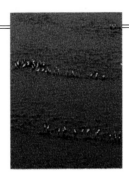

CRANE RIVER

THE PERFECT PLATTE

The Platte is actually three rivers. Two of them, the North Platte and South Platte, arise as meltwaters high in the Colorado Rockies. They plunge down steep mountain gorges, gathering bulk and picking up a load of sediment before spilling across the level plains of central Nebraska. There, the two streams combine to become the Platte. The resultant river runs east, eventually joining the Missouri River near Omaha.

Sandhill cranes were named for the gently rolling hills lying on the north edge of the Platte River Valley in east-central Nebraska. The sandhills, which are sand dunes tenuously stabilized by a fragile, grassy epidermis, are not crane habitat. A better name for the birds might be "Platte cranes," because the mid-continental flock of sandhills is critically dependent upon North America's only perfect crane river.

That notion isn't easy for modern visitors to understand. In most places, the Platte looks like an ordinary prairie river. It does not appear to be a river whose unique properties are crucial to the future of sandhill cranes. Nor does it look environmentally abused. Yet it is both.

THE HISTORIC PLATTE

White explorers were astonished when they first beheld the Platte about

The Platte: An area that's crucial to sandhills.

a century and a half ago. The river was unreal, bizarre, a "burlesque of all the rivers in the world."

"The river is a perfect curiosity," wrote a pioneer woman in 1859. "It is so very different from any of our streams that it is hard to realize that a river should be running so near the top of the ground without any timber, and no bank at all." The Platte often appeared to run above the surrounding terrain like a milkshake spilled on a counter top. It seemed to be—and almost was—a river with no banks.

It was also a river with no streamside trees. Wrote one emigrant: "There is no timber growing upon the margin of the river, not even a willow switch." The only trees to be seen were growing on the larger of the Platte's many small islands, islands sometimes compared to emeralds in a gold setting.

Even the water was unusual. The golden tint of the Platte resulted from all the glacial till, gravel, and sand that the river carried down from its violent birthplace in the Rockies. An emigrant who scooped up a cup of the stuff found that the bottom fourth of the cup settled hours later into solid mud. In spring, at least, the Platte wasn't so much flowing water as a broad slurry of sand and gravel "too thick to drink and too thin to plow."

What was most impressive about the Platte was its odd profile. "Miles wide and inches deep" was the catch phrase,

and it wasn't much of an exaggeration. Careful measurements put the width of the original Platte at two miles in some areas. Yet the river could be forded at almost any point that wasn't guarded by the notorious bubbling "quicksand" bottoms. The early Platte reminded pioneers of the sea.

Hydrologists call shallow, multi-channeled streams like the Platte "braided rivers," referring to the many twisting channels that resemble the braids of a rope. The Platte was once a restless, dynamic river that continually threw up new sandbars, reamed out fresh channels, and generally redefined itself in a cataclysmic gush each spring.

CRANE RIVER

What made the Platte unique also made it seem specifically designed for cranes. As if by divine plan, North America's only perfect crane river was positioned geographically just where it should be in order to support cranes at the most vulnerable moment in their annual cycle.

Cranes must prepare themselves for three great energy drains in spring. The first is the effort of traveling to breeding grounds as distant as Siberia. Secondly, mated females must produce eggs, a process placing unique demands on their bodies. And finally, breeding pairs must sacrifice their own nutritional needs throughout the lengthy

Preceding pages: A panoramic view of cranes roosting on America's only perfect crane river.

brooding period.

As a result, adult cranes need a surplus of nutrition in spring that will build up reserves of energy for the weeks ahead. Each nesting crane must acquire fat reserves of about ten percent of its body weight—almost a pound. That's the equivalent of a 150-pound human gaining about 20 pounds in a month.

The caloric requirement is easily supplied by waste grain found along the Platte. Before middle America was brought under cultivation, crane numbers were limited by the amount of spring food available. That limitation no longer holds. This is one change— probably the *only* one—brought about by humans that has benefited sandhills. Today's sandhills never need to fly farther than about eight miles from the Platte to find all the grain they require.

Of course, the cranes could find grain along just about any other midwestern river. But they need something else that is much harder to find. Sandhills spend about a third of their daylight hours feeding in the floodplain wet meadows adjacent to the Platte. There, cranes consume a variety of animal foods—primarily snails, snail shells, worms, and insects. The animal food offers what biologists consider the cranes' only reliable source of dietary protein and calcium, necessary for egg and embryo formation.

Even experts don't totally understand the complex hydrological relationships connecting the river to its wet meadows. The Platte Valley contains a variety of grassy areas linked to the river by the porous gravel substrate. The water table in the meadows rises and falls with river levels. Formerly, the wet meadows flooded in spring, then dried and became heavily vegetated in summer. Each spring flood would inundate the meadows again, decomposing dead plant material. That material became the base of a food chain supporting snails and other animals. At the top of the chain stood the crane.

The bizarre, broad-but-shallow profile of the Platte was uniquely ideal for crane roosting. Sandhills are fastidious in their choice of roosting habitat. They will not roost in confined circumstances where they are vulnerable to predation. Sandhills seek a river channel at least 1,000 feet wide, and prefer an even less constricted area. They want ample sandbars submerged no deeper than six inches, with little or no in-stream vegetation. Any predator would have to make a long, splashy attack to reach a crane sleeping on such a sandbar.

The Platte's location makes it ideal for spring staging. The Big Bend stretch lies close to the geographical center of North America, halfway between the Gulf Coast and the wetland regions near the U.S.-Canada border, where the birds can rest and feed.

In short, the Platte is the only river in North America offering cranes just what they need in spring. Where else could the birds go? The Missouri is too deep, and has no wet meadows. The Loup and Niobrara rivers lack the expansive size, shallow sandbars, and wet meadow complexes of the Platte. According to Craig Faanes, a crane specialist working for the U.S. Fish and Wildlife Service, "The cranes can't go somewhere else. There *is* nothing else like the Platte. It is here or nothing for the birds."

Faanes (known fondly as "the bird man of the Platte" by thousands of school children who have experienced his educational presentations) says, "The Platte is the bottleneck, the crucial link in the cranes' survival. The limits of crane habitat on the Platte are the limiting factor in sandhill crane populations."

CHANGES AND THREATS

The link between crane futures and the Platte would not be alarming if the Platte's crane habitat were secure. But it is not. Like many other western rivers, the Platte is now in danger of becoming an oxymoron—a "river" without water. Over 40 dams in Colorado, Wyoming, and Nebraska tame its formerly wild flows. Water that would otherwise flood the Platte's grassy meadows is being sucked off through irrigation pipes to raise a water-loving crop (corn) in an arid region.

The net effect of all these water projects has been the removal of 70 percent of the river's natural, historic flow. Statistics are bland things that rarely communicate the gritty reality of environmental threats, yet these numbers speak with eloquence: Four-fifths of the world's sandhill cranes are critically dependent on a stretch of river that has lost almost three-fourths of its water.

A plethora of agencies are currently scrapping for the right to make further withdrawals from the remaining 30 percent of the Platte's water flow. Approximately 14 additional water projects are under consideration as of this writing. If all are approved, they will consume 80 percent of what is left of the Platte. Conservationists are forced to fight a complicated, multi-front battle. Victories are hard-won and tentative. Each time a project is defeated, it comes back in several new forms, like a science fiction monster that simply multiplies each time it's slain.

Water projects already built have caused several disturbing difficulties within crane habitat. The river is shrinking. Channel widths have been reduced by as much as 90 percent in some stretches used by cranes. A river that once reminded people of the sea now looks, in many areas, like a common farmland stream. Even if no more water is withdrawn, the projects already in place continue to propel changes that degrade crane habitat.

The unruly spring flows that gave the Platte its character are now trapped behind concrete walls. Any water escaping the irrigators is meted out at steady rates too feeble to drive a dynamic, braided river. Sediment-free river flows now wash sandbars away, rather than creating new ones. Moderate stream flows can't scour vegetation from the river's bed as they once did.

Crane habitat is most severely threatened by encroaching vegetation. In particular, willows sprout like weeds on islands and banks. As young trees gain a foothold, they stabilize the banks and make them more hospitable for other colonizing vegetation. Willows and cottonwoods are now rooted securely enough to force the formerly incorrigible river to respect its own banks.

The wet meadows are drying up. The Platte no longer floods the adjacent low-lying areas each spring. And since the river is now cutting itself a channel like those of typical rivers, it no longer runs near the surface of the land, so the water table of the region is dropping.

Much of the old wet meadow acreage is simply gone. Many floodplain acres are now in cultivation, adding to the nation's surplus of field corn. Sand and gravel mining destroyed some formerly wet meadows. Overall, only 25 percent of the original wet meadow complexes remain.

The manmade changes have severely pinched the amount of suitable roosting habitat available to sandhills. Where approximately 200 miles of the Platte once offered sandhills safe roosts and food-rich adjacent meadows, only about 80 miles now meet the birds' most basic requirements.

Vegetative encroachment is progressing from west to east, so cranes have been forced to move eastward in order to find suitable roosting areas. The birds have also been attracted eastward by limited stretches of the river that are under the intensive management of the Audubon's Rowe Sanctuary and the Platte River Whooping Crane Trust. Major stretches of the river that hosted multitudes of whinnying cranes as recently as the 1960s now stand empty each spring.

More and more cranes are being packed into a smaller area, which presents several threats to the sandhills and their endangered whooping crane cousins. Crowding may have adverse impacts on social organization, pair bonding, and reproductive success.

Above all, biologists fear that crowding could result in a disease epidemic. Just as cholera once haunted the Platte's emigrant trains, avian cholera seems poised to ravage the crowded mid-continental sandhill crane flock. Cholera outbreaks in the nearby Rainwater Basin have taken a heavy toll on ducks and geese. In a new and ominous phenomenon, scientists have begun to find the bodies of sandhills that died of cholera. Crowding might or might not increase the susceptibility of cranes to cholera, but it certainly creates a grim scenario in which any cholera outbreak could destroy a large percentage of the world's sandhills. Given the limited reproductive potential of sandhills, a single major cholera event occurring while the cranes are massed could be calamitous.

The crane-inhabited stretch of the Platte River has been referred to as the waist of a habitat hourglass. Cranes flow into the Big Bend from a broad geographical region. Weeks later, they spread out over sparsely populated breeding grounds. At no other moment in their lives are sandhills as concentrated and vulnerable as they are during their stay along the Platte. The future of the mid-continental sandhill flock is virtually synonymous with the future of the river.

MANAGING FOR CRANES

Intensive management has reversed the destruction of crane habitat in two land holdings along the Platte.

The Platte River Whooping Crane

Trust was set up in 1979 as a court-mandated "mitigation" measure to compensate for the environmental damage expected to result from the construction of the Grayrocks Reservoir in Wyoming. The court's decree establishes the Trust's mission: to protect and maintain the viability of its lands for migratory birds. The court arranged for a one-time payment of $7.5 million, and interest from that fund provides most of the Crane Trust's operating budget.

Since its creation, the Crane Trust has enjoyed exceptionally effective leadership from its director, John VanDerWalker. By practicing a "good neighbor" policy, VanderWalker has reversed some of the ill will created by a heavy-handed U.S. Fish and Wildlife effort to buy up crane habitat in the 1970s. Without being antagonistic, VanDerWalker has been an effective advocate for wildlife.

The Trust channels most of its resources into three efforts. One is a habitat acquisition and management program. Long-range plans call for the establishment of ten habitat sites spaced along the 80-mile Big Bend stretch. Management of these sites would give cranes the space, the isolation from humans, and the floodplain wet meadows they require. Completing this project will require as long as two decades, but the work is well underway. In its first ten years, the Crane Trust purchased more than 8,000 acres of land, including over 16 miles of river frontage. The largest purchase so far is 4,500 acres of habitat near Grand Island. Vegetation is being cleared away from several miles of river channel by heavy machinery. The Trust has restored nine miles of crane roosting habitat and 200 acres of grassland.

A second major program involves researching the hydrology of the Platte River Valley. This entails development of computer models to show just what water flows are necessary to preserve crane habitat. According to Gary Lingle, avian ecologist for the Trust, "We're trying to determine what flows are necessary to maintain the viability of these wet meadows." Before legal arguments can be made for altering dam "flow regimes," conservationists must acquire hard data about water flows, and the Trust has been gathering that data.

Trust spokesmen maintain that even a Platte depleted by 70 percent could provide crane habitat if flow regimes could be modified to accommodate wildlife values. The Trust has also documented that the presently used irrigation systems are very wasteful. If they were made more efficient, the Trust contends, "There is enough water to maintain existing irrigation uses *and* restore the river."

A third major effort of the Trust involves representing the interests of

wildlife in battles now raging over the renewal of operating permits for dams already in place on the Platte. Permits are good for 50 years. The first to come up for review is the permit for the McConaughy Reservoir project, created by the Kingsley Dam (coincidentally, one of the most damaging projects to crane habitat). People on both sides of the issue realize the McConaughy debate will set precedents for the 320 or so permits that will be reviewed in the future. In the eyes of the Trust, the review of McConaughy is a "once-in-half-a-century" opportunity to attain balanced management of the river.

Federal legislation passed after most dams were built specifies that wildlife values should be considered equally with irrigation and hydropower interests before a dam is licensed for another five decades. That gives a two-against-one advantage to economic interests, but at least wildlife concerns must be considered as a matter of law. These legal battles might determine whether the mid-continental population of sandhills has a secure future.

The second major organization maintaining crane habitat along the Platte is the Audubon Society.

The background of this effort is unusual. In 1971, a spinster named Lillian Annette Rowe died in New Jersey. She apparently had accumulated a sizable estate by living frugally on her schoolteacher's salary. One of Rowe's interests was parrot behavior. Her will specified that her estate monies be used either to publish a book she was writing on parrots, or for "establishing a bird sanctuary anywhere in the nation." Fortunately for cranes, Rowe's parrot book was incomplete, so her bequest became available for use in creating a sanctuary.

At that moment, the Audubon Society was engaged in a legal battle to save Platte River crane habitat. In 1973, the Society used the Rowe bequest to purchase 782 acres of prime crane habitat along the Platte, downstream from Grand River. The holding now includes 1,000 acres, much of it grassy meadow. Rowe apparently never saw the Platte or, for that matter, a crane. Yet her name is permanently linked to efforts to preserve the world's most important sandhill population.

Rowe managers fight a never-ending battle against willows, box elders, cottonwoods, and hackberry trees. Rooted trees are cleared by hand, only to rise again like crabgrass on a well-watered lawn. Grassy meadows along the Platte are maintained as natural prairie by staging controlled burns.

Like Trust managers, the Rowe managers are discovering that they can't maintain wet meadows without wetness. Expensive hand labor can hold back encroaching willows, but without water, the grassy meadows lose their value to cranes. A river-based ecosystem cannot survive without the river that sustains it.

LOOKING AHEAD

The future of the Platte and the cranes that depend upon it remains very much in doubt. Optimists find grounds for hope, primarily in the relicensing hearings and the declining profitability of Great Plains agriculture. But pessimists find grounds for despair, primarily in the precarious position of the river and the continuing indifference of local public opinion toward wildlife.

The issue is being contended almost daily in grinding, never-ending legal battles that pit conservationists against powerful economic interests, sandhills against cornfields, and whooping cranes against hydropower.

Tracks in the sand: Are the cranes walking into a secure future?

THE CRY OF
THE SANDHILL

INTERNATIONAL CRANE FOUNDATION

It was inevitable that Ron Sauey and George Archibald would become friends when they met as graduate students at Cornell University. Both were already ardent students of cranes. And, as the two young men talked, they developed a shared dream: to create an institution whose mission would be saving the world's cranes.

Dreams—even improbable dreams—sometimes come true. When Sauey's parents vacated a horse farm near Baraboo, Wisconsin, they offered to lease the land to the two young friends for one dollar a year. Archibald and Sauey converted old stables and barns into crane housing, enlisted volunteer staffing, and contacted zoos around the world with an unusual query: "Do you have any cranes to lend?" The International Crane Foundation was in business.

From the start, the ICF's goals have been to promote five essential activities: crane research, education, habitat protection, captive breeding, and restocking. While all of the activities were important, the crane center was in a particularly advantageous position to promote innovative research on captive breeding and restocking.

As time went on, Archibald and Sauey increasingly turned their efforts toward forming a unique international network of crane devotees, students,

---

Animal behaviorist Rob Horwich in his crane costume: Would sandhill chicks accept this thing as their mother?

scientists, and governmental officials on the five continents where cranes reside. They soon saw their work producing results, in the form of crane conservation programs, preserves, and research.

After seven years at the old horse farm, the founders realized that the ICF needed better quarters. The foundation bought 160 acres of land five miles north of the Sauey farm. A physical plant specifically designed to serve as a crane foundation was built, and the last crane was moved into the new quarters in 1989.

The ICF's attractive new facilities are divided between public and private functions. Many of the cranes are housed in Crane City, a distinct area that provides the birds with privacy and security. Much of the important genetic work is done there.

Other facilities entertain and inform the visitors who come from all over the world. One zoo-like area allows visitors to observe all 15 of the world's cranes. Volunteer guides lead the guests on informative tours. Visitors enjoy the bookstore and theater. Walking paths wind through the ICF's rolling meadow grounds, which are now being restored to natural prairie. A favorite activity is

Preceding pages: An overview of Crane City. Above: The two dreamers, Sauey and Archibald.

the "chick walk." Visitors stroll along as an ICF volunteer leads a tame crane chick out to forage in the adjacent meadows, communicating with the chick via trilling chirrups.

An odd publicity breakthrough for the newly founded ICF came about when Archibald began dancing with a whooping crane named Tex. One of the ICF's missions is to maintain a genetic bank for different species. Tex, a female, was the sole survivor from a group of hand-reared cranes. Because she survived stresses fatal to other whooping cranes, Tex possessed genes that might benefit her species. But she was imprinted on human beings, and would not mate with whooping cranes. Even when artificially inseminated, Tex would not produce eggs, because she had not experienced the normal crane social mating rituals.

Thus the dancing. Archibald speculated that Tex would lay eggs if she were artificially inseminated *and* encouraged to breed by dancing. For six weeks in spring, Archibald spent every waking hour keeping Tex company and dancing with her. The spectacle of a man dancing with a crane caught the public's fancy. It looked ludicrous at first, yet there was pathos in the plight

By dancing with Tex and keeping her company, George Archibald induced the whooping crane to lay an important egg.

of a whooping crane doomed to be a stranger to her own kind. All across the country, people watched Archibald and Tex dancing on television shows. Tex was eventually killed by a raccoon that penetrated the ICF's security system, but not before she made two precious contributions—a great deal of publicity for the ICF and Gee Whiz, a young whooping crane that carries Tex's remarkable genes.

Ron Sauey died unexpectedly in 1987. His legacy remains in the form of the Ron Sauey Memorial Library for crane research, and in all the crane programs around the world that he helped establish.

The sandhill is only one of 15 crane species about which the ICF is concerned. As a relatively secure crane, the sandhill might not seem to warrant as much interest as the endangered whooping crane or the mysterious black-necked crane. Yet the sandhill plays a vital role in ICF activities precisely because its population is large. Sandhills serve as test animals—guinea pigs, if you will—for experiments that might save endangered crane species.

CROSS-FOSTERING

Cross-fostering is a restocking technique through which whooping crane eggs are placed under a wild sandhill mother. For 17 years, the program was a major part of the federal effort to restore whooping cranes.

The eggs came from wild whoopers nesting in Wood Buffalo Park in Canada, and from captive whooping cranes at the Patuxent Wildlife Research Center in Laurel, Maryland. The eggs were placed under wild greater sandhills at Gray's Lake National Wildlife Refuge in Idaho. Taking eggs from wild whooping cranes didn't hurt the population, because whooping cranes almost never succeed at raising a pair of young. Thus, one egg was expendable. To acquire an egg, Canadian biologists descended from the sky in a helicopter, rushed out, and grabbed one. Remarkably, this noisy and violent nest-robbing didn't cause whooping cranes to abandon their nests.

Cross-fostering has failed, through no fault of the sandhill mothers. In all, 209 whooping crane eggs were placed under sandhills. Only 84 hatched. Of those, only 13 adults survive today.

Two things apparently went wrong. Mortality was exceptionally high at Gray's Lake among all age classes of cranes. Water levels were low, leaving the cranes highly vulnerable to coyote predation. The cranes that survived the coyotes often crashed into the thicket of power lines surrounding the refuge. In short, a number of habitat problems at Gray's Lake sabotaged the cross-fostering program's chances.

However, the program may have

been doomed for other reasons. Whooping cranes reared by sandhill mothers have not reproduced. They are whooping cranes physically and genetically, but not socially. Perhaps they can't pair with whooping cranes because they have imprinted on a sandhill mother. The socio-sexual aspect of crane biology is apparently more complex and important than researchers had anticipated.

The overall effort to restore the whooping crane isn't helped much by creating sexually dysfunctional birds. The cross-fostering program has been discontinued.

ISOLATION REARING

Many young creatures imprint on the first large, moving object they see after birth. This useful mechanism normally bonds the young one to its mother. But when the first moving thing an infant beholds is not its mother, or even one of its own species, things go awry. Most of us first learned about that in the nursery rhyme, "Mary Had a Little Lamb."

Thus, when Dayton Hyde rescued an abandoned sandhill egg, he knew he was committed to playing mother to a sandhill chick. Over the years, many

Workers separate two whooping crane siblings, preventing them from "charging" at one another.

crane eggs have been hatched under similar circumstances. Such a bird was Tex, Archibald's dancing partner. Like Tex, these birds grow up identifying with human beings.

By using a technique called isolation rearing, it's possible to rear a chick without causing it to imprint on humans. The key lies in preventing the young crane from seeing its human keepers. The chick is kept in a brooding box equipped with a one-way mirror, and fed through an opening with a hand puppet that looks like a crane.

The puppets used at the ICF are convincing facsimiles of a crane's head. A large pair of shears acts as the mouth. Naturalistic upper and lower bills are attached to the blades. The keeper's hand in the puppet operates the mouth by working the shears.

A variation of this basic procedure is being used at the Patuxent Wildlife Research Center. There, the crane chick's brooding area has one open, wire-mesh wall. A crane of the appropriate species is kept on the other side, to help socialize the chick.

COSTUMED MOTHERS AND SOFT RELEASES

Isolation rearing prevents inappropriate imprinting, but in the process it creates something sad—a young crane with no mother or father. Because the ultimate product of artificially rearing

chicks should be the release of a bird capable of living and breeding normally, the ICF felt that isolation rearing technology needed improvement.

A major advancement in the technology resulted from a collaboration between the ICF and Rob Horwich, an animal behaviorist with a special interest in psychological development. The crane chosen for this experiment was the most available species, the sandhill.

Horwich invented a new and more comprehensive experimental rearing protocol by adding a sandhill taxidermy mount to the brooding quarters, and by piping in the vocalizations that sandhill mothers make to their chicks. He also invented a grey, sandhill-colored costume for keepers. The costume was hot, hard to see out of, and undeniably weird, but it hid the keeper's face and human identity. The keeper in the costume wore a sandhill puppet head on one hand.

There were questions. Would the chicks accept this *thing* as their mother? Would they spot the human under the cloth? Would they ignore the keeper's cloaked head and accept a mother who wore her head on her wing? Could the poor keeper who had to run about flapping and croaking in this bizarre garb ever live down the ridicule of fellow workers?

The first thrill for Horwich came when, dressed in the mother costume, he entered the brooding quarters of his

A "surrogate mother" comforts a crane chick.

first test sandhill. The chick instantly tried to nestle under him, just as it would its mother. The chick came when Horwich called. At last, the little sandhill had a mother.

Horwich hoped the costumed mother could teach chicks some of the lessons that wild chicks learn from their parents. The costumed mother showed chicks how to probe for food and go after insects. Horwich taught his charges to dig up arrowhead tubers, and he introduced them to field corn.

Some lessons were more tricky. To make the chicks wary of humans, Horwich had an accomplice charge at them while roaring viciously. This was only partially effective. The test chicks didn't truly fear humans until they were later taught to do so by wild cranes. And when teaching his chicks to fly, Horwich could go only so far.

Once they were flying, it was time to introduce the colts to wild cranes. Horwich took his charges to Necedah, a marsh not far north of the ICF where wild greater sandhills stage on their way south. Horwich camped in a tent, and the young cranes were penned in a corral. The colts flew out to join wild cranes each day, returning periodically to the security of the cloth mother.

When the colts were just over three months old, the costume was retired. The young sandhills suddenly found themselves orphans. After some confusion and hesitation, they cast their lot with the wild birds.

The "soft release" program (so-called because the release is gradual) was next taken up by field biologist Richard Urbanek. Over the next several years, he reared and released many more young sandhills, using the same basic techniques. When some of his young cranes strayed from the wild flocks, Urbanek tracked them down, called them in with the costume, and reintroduced them to the wild flock. Urbanek has been able to extend this control to an amazing degree, using the costume to call in cranes after they've spent two years in the wild.

Urbanek's main innovation was to separate his colts into several small groups at release time. The separation prevented them from forming a large flock of puppet-reared cranes that didn't know where to migrate.

Before these experiments, experts thought the best candidates for release were one- or two-year old cranes. The survival rates of such birds were "good" if half survived the winter migration. But much younger soft-released cranes have been surviving at rates of 85 to 90 percent. Urbanek's soft-released colts have returned to his Michigan marsh at an astounding rate of 100 percent.

Best of all, some of the offspring of the cloth mother have now paired with wild sandhills, and are poised to raise families of their own. This technique might re-establish sandhill flocks in regions they haven't inhabited for a long time. Researchers also hope soft-released whooping cranes will soon socialize and mate with wild whoopers. Perhaps the great project aimed at restoring wild, breeding whooping cranes is about to produce results.

Cloth-mothering a sandhill chick is hard work, and mothering two chicks is agony during the period when they relentlessly attack each other. Later, just before transferring their bonds to wild cranes, the chicks regress and grow so dependent upon their mother that they become "terrible little pests" according to Horwich.

There are compensations. ICF cloth mothers have been astonished at the rush of maternal affection they occasionally feel for their charges. As Urbanek puts it, "These are my kids. What more can I say? This work is my life, and these are my kids!"

Seeing the colts fly for the first time is a thrill, but nothing matches the joy of scanning a multitude of staging cranes with binoculars and spotting the chicks, alive and mixing casually with wild birds. Then the keeper can say with justifiable pride, "I was a good mother."

The soft release program is the *only* broad-scale effort to rear and release cranes that function naturally in the wild. A program criticized by some experts as loony and unscientific might be the most sophisticated rearing technique and the best hope for restoring endangered crane populations.

HUNTING

The hunting of cranes, once popular, was banned in 1916 with the signing of the Migratory Bird Treaty. Crane hunting became legal again in limited areas in 1961. Now, the mid-continental sandhills are hunted within Alaska, Canada, Mexico and most states of the Central Flyway.

The season has been controversial from the start. Because cranes have low reproductive potential, crane fans worry that hunting mortality might be too heavy to be offset by natural recruitment. The U.S. Fish and Wildlife Service acknowledged that concern when it determined that no more than five percent of the fall crane population could be safely harvested. By contrast, harvest rates of 20 percent for fall populations of ducks have been considered safe.

Critics of crane hunting have not been reassured by the low harvest target. Setting seasons to achieve specific harvest levels is part science, part art. Mistakes happen. And when the target harvest is such a low number, small mistakes can have major impacts, because the margin for error is so small.

The difficulty of getting reliable census data makes mistakes more likely. If the strength of a population is not

Overleaf: Neither the Pied Piper nor a sandpiper, Rob Horwich is a crane mother leading her charges into the marshland.

known with precision—and it's not in the case of these sandhills—managers can't be sure that their hunting regulations are truly conservative.

A number of techniques for counting the cranes of the mid-continental flock have been tried and found inaccurate. The newest technique involves sending an F-16 fighter jet screaming at low altitudes along the Platte at night, with infrared cameras whirring. This must startle the sandhills considerably, but it yields a picture of every crane on the river. The technique is better than those used earlier, but is not as accurate as it needs to be for prudent management. The switch in census techniques makes it harder to trace long-term trends, since the sets of data are not comparable.

There are other complications. The population of greater sandhills needs no reduction. Until recently, the Rocky Mountain flock of greaters was classified as "threatened." The hunting seasons intended to control populations of lesser sandhills sometimes result in the killing of other subtypes. Some observers believe hunters selectively target the larger birds whenever large and small subtypes share the same habitat.

All of this puts a burden on the season-setters. After consulting detailed migration data, they juggle season dates and locations in an effort to expose only the lesser sandhills to the guns.

Predictably, those who set the seasons claim they can do this with precision. Predictably, those who detest crane hunting believe serious mistakes are being made.

When crane seasons were first opened, most hunters regarded cranes as a "trophy" species, and hunted them infrequently. Now, it seems that more hunters are learning how to hunt sandhills. Mail-order sporting catalogs are beginning to advertise sandhill crane calls and decoys. Local guides are promoting sandhill hunts. If sandhill hunting becomes more popular, or if hunters become more proficient, the seasons may need further limitation.

Fortunately, the latest and most reliable information on survival rates among the mid-continental birds is reassuring. The nation's largest flock of sandhills has been increasing steadily at about two percent a year. But clearly, crane hunting requires most careful monitoring.

THE FUTURE OF SANDHILLS

Aldo Leopold was by nature an optimistic man. Yet it seems he concluded that sandhills were fated to disappear:

Some day . . . the last crane will trumpet his farewell and spiral skyward from the great marsh. High out of the clouds will fall the sound of hunting horns, the baying of the phantom pack, the tinkle of little bells, and then a silence never to be broken, unless perchance in some far pasture of the Milky Way.

Leopold's fears were based on tragic fact. He had seen Wisconsin's population of sandhills fall to 25 nesting pairs in 1936. He could not have anticipated that a thousand sandhills would be nesting in Wisconsin four decades later.

Over and over, the sandhill has proven itself to be a flexible, opportunistic, and durable species. We can only guess at what apocalyptic changes it has witnessed and adjusted to during its nine million years on the continent. The ultimate survivor of the bird world, the sandhill has withstood every conceivable test except one. Humans and their unique forms of economic aggression represent a threat that even sandhills might not be able to withstand.

But to put the case that way is to invert reality. The real issue is not whether sandhills survive human rapaciousness, but whether humans will make a few adjustments in their activities in order to secure a future for the sandhills.

What is being tested is the quality of the American soul. Either this society will preserve a moderate amount of living space for cranes or we will not. According to the Platte River Whooping Crane Trust, there is no irreconcilable gap between environmental policies favoring humans and those favoring sandhill cranes. It might be environmentally foolish to raise corn in arid regions, but people can do so and still preserve sandhill populations by making adjustments in dam flow regimes.

The United States practices a bizarre reverse triage with respect to wildlife. Rather than allocating resources where they will do the most good for the most important species, we push wildlife to the brink of extinction, then marshall enormous resources in frantic efforts to undo the damage. If the Platte is "managed" that way, then America's most important sandhill flock will be in grave trouble sooner or later.

The various sandhill subtypes face highly variable futures. The extremely endangered Cuban subtype will probably be lost if current trends hold. The Mississippi sandhill is in a tenuous position, but seems to be more than holding its own. Its fate rests mostly with researchers endeavoring to bolster its numbers. The Florida subtype seems secure, and is currently expanding its population.

The greater sandhill might see increases in the next years. With moderate losses due to hunting and abundant migration route food, the limiting factor on this group seems to be the amount of secure nesting habitat. These majestic cranes might be restored to ancients haunts where sandhill unison calls haven't been heard in this century. Whenever a marshy refuge of any size is created in the Great Lakes states, a sandhill couple wings in before long and makes the refuge ring with strident territorial claims.

So the voice of the sandhill has not been silenced. The same spooky cry that echoed across primeval marshes can be heard today. The cry carries a simple message. It says: *"I'm still here!"*

May it always be so.

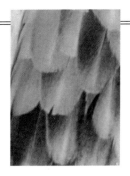

APPENDIX A:
CRANES OF THE WORLD

Cranes are the most prominent members of the order of Gruiformes. Other Gruiformes include the limpkin, rails, gallinules, and coots. The limpkin is in the *Aramidae* family. Coots, rails and gallinules are in the *Rallidae* family. Cranes are in the *Gruidae* family.

The largest genus within the *Gruidae* family is *Grus*, which includes the sandhill and nine other species. The *Grus* birds are considered more highly evolved than *Balearica* cranes such as the crowned cranes of Africa. The *Grus* genus name derives from the Greek name for cranes—*geranos* or *gereunos*—and is probably an onomatopoeic rendition of crane calls.

The international crane family numbers either 14 or 15 species, depending on whether the grey crowned and black crowned cranes are counted as one or two species. The crane clan includes of some of the most beautiful, varied, and intriguing birds on earth. Unfortunately, many face uncertain futures.

BLACK-NECKED CRANE

A bird of the remote high country, this mysterious crane has a gray body, black flight feathers, black neck, and a black head with a red forehead. It breeds in the wetlands of Tibet and winters in limited areas of India, Bhutan, and southwestern China. The black-necked crane was the last of the world's species to be identified. It is considered the least-known of all

The black-necked crane, the least-known of all cranes.

cranes and one of the least-known of birds. One male black-necked residing at the International Crane Foundation weighs just over 14 pounds; one female was weighed at 12 pounds.

These rare cranes dwindled during several decades in which Asian wildlife needs were largely ignored. Now the birds are receiving careful attention from Chinese scientists, and a winter sanctuary has been created for them. The population was recently estimated at 4,000.

BLUE CRANE

The blue crane can puff up its cheeks until its head resembles a cobra's. By contrast, most cranes indicate excitement by exhibiting a red forehead. Blue cranes have grey-blue bodies and necks, with a long, dark, pheasant-like "tail" (actually not a tail, but an extension of the secondary wing feathers). The upper half of the head is white, and the bill is unusually short for a crane. Males weigh about 12 pounds.

The blue crane, the national bird of South Africa, migrates short distances seasonally, though almost all blue cranes live in South Africa throughout the year. The blue crane often feeds among springbok antelope, in a symbiotic relationship that provides food for the cranes and "watch-crane" protection for the antelope. The blue crane

population has declined abruptly in recent decades, due to the destruction of its grassland habitat. In protecting their crops, farmers poison large numbers of cranes. Fans of these lovely and unusual cranes are organizing to improve the bird's future prospects. Blue cranes now number about 5,000.

BROLGA

The name of this crane, which is possibly onomatopoeic, comes from the aboriginal people of Australia. In fact, the brolga is frequently called the Australian crane.

The brolga hybridizes with its close relative, the sarus crane. Brolgas live on a broad range of marshy land in Australia, plus a tiny portion of New Guinea. The adults are blue-grey with dark grey primaries (the long feathers on the outer portion of the wing). The crown is unfeathered and dark green in color. The red usually found on the forehead of *Grus* cranes seems to have been pushed back on the head and cheeks of brolgas. They have a small, dark pouch under their chins, and males weigh 16 pounds.

Brolgas are tough, resourceful, and adaptable birds. They seem to reproduce at a higher rate than most cranes. Brolgas are considered "secure" at present, though they face competition from sarus cranes.

The blue crane: It shows excitement by puffing up its cheeks.

THE CROWNED CRANES

The black crowned and grey crowned cranes are the most glamorous cranes in the world. Their jaunty crowns are replicated in African dance costumes. Crowned cranes, which lack the elongated trachea of the *Grus* cranes, are thought to be the only survivors of a more primitive type of crane that was eventually displaced by the *Grus*. Evolved to thrive in near-tropical conditions, these *Balearica* cranes have not fared well as the world's climate has become progressively cooler over many centuries. The crowned cranes are among the most beautiful "living fossils" in the world.

Some authorities do classify the crowned cranes as two species, while others consider them subtypes of a single species. They are the only cranes with a grasping hind toe that allows them to roost in trees. Crowned cranes have dark bodies, exotic golden crowns, and bright white cheeks. Their wing coverts are white, shading to the same lovely straw gold found on their crowns. The cheek patch of the black crowned crane is red and white. The more common grey crowned crane has a white cheek patch and a red wattle.

Above: The tough, adaptable brolga crane. Right: The crowned crane, which pays a high price for its beauty.

Both have short, stout bills. They are among the world's smaller cranes, weighing only about eight pounds.

These stunning birds live in open-country grasslands near water in several regions of Africa. The grey crowned crane lives year-round in southeastern Africa. While under pressure from expanding human populations, it is not currently endangered. The black crowned crane lives in the Sahel region (south of the Sahara) and has been hurt directly and indirectly by recent droughts. These cranes pay a high price for their beauty, as they are frequently trapped and sold. Conservationists are concerned about their future.

DEMOISELLE CRANE

Meaning "lovely lady," the name of this small crane was supposedly bestowed by another lovely lady—Marie Antoinette. Demoiselles are found in grassland, not marshland. Demoiselles and blue cranes are the only species with no red on their heads. Though they differ in appearance, the two are closely related.

The demoiselle has a grey body with a black neck and head. A white line starts behind the eye, carries on past

The demoiselle, or "lovely lady."

the ears, and becomes a delicate plume. The bill is short. The long neck feathers dangle gracefully in the manner of the egret's throat feathers. This is the smallest crane in the world, with males weighing less than five pounds.

Demoiselles have the widest range of all cranes, nesting from the Black Sea to Mongolia and wintering in India, Pakistan, and the Sahel of Africa. Relatively little is known about the breeding grounds of demoiselles. These gregarious cranes build their nests by using stones instead of vegetation, and their speckled eggs are hard to discern among the stones. Although expanding human agriculture has shrunk the original range of this bird, the demoiselle is considered abundant and secure.

EURASIAN CRANE

Europe's only crane nests from Great Britain to Siberia, and winters from Morocco to Egypt, Iran, India, and China. It's often called the common crane. The Eurasian is considered the closest relative of the whooping crane. These dark grey birds have very dark necks and heads that contrast sharply with a broad white stripe beginning behind the eyes and extending down the nape. The unfeathered crown is red. Males weigh about 12 pounds.

Eurasian cranes might once have nested as far west as Ireland. Over the centuries, the birds have lost a great deal of habitat, particularly in Europe. Yet at the same time, legions of crane fans have worked to establish food plots and safe stopover points for their cranes. Continued efforts of that sort should assure a future for this highly adaptable species.

HOODED CRANE

The nesting habits of these small cranes have been difficult to study because they nest in inaccessible regions of Siberia. Most hooded cranes winter in Japan, where they are revered and closely studied. The hooded crane

The Eurasian, Europe's only crane.

is mostly dark gray, with a very distinctive white head and neck and an unfeathered red crown. Males weigh over nine pounds.

Relatively little is known about how much habitat this crane has lost. The first nest wasn't located until 140 years after the species had been identified. Though endangered, the hooded crane seems to have increased its numbers in recent years, partly because of food made available at Japanese wintering areas. The most important winter flock now numbers about 7,000 birds. Nonetheless, authorities fear that hooded cranes could be lost unless international cooperation results in the preservation of secure habitat.

RED-CROWNED CRANE

This majestic bird is often called the Japanese crane. It nests in Siberia, northern China, and Japan, wintering in southern China and the unpopulated demilitarized zone between North and South Korea. There's also a resident flock on the northern Japanese island of Hokkaido. The red-crowned is an elegant crane, almost all white but with black secondaries and a black band on the neck and lower head. The naked crown is red. The red-crowned weighs as much as 25 pounds, making it the heaviest crane in the world. Many consider the red-crowned the world's most beautiful crane.

Despite its special standing in Japanese culture, the red-crowned crane has been hurt by rapidly expanding human populations in its wintering areas. The crane is officially classified as "vulnerable." International cooperation between biologists should help improve the bird's prospects. Some authorities regard this species as the second-rarest crane (after the North American whooping crane), while others feel the Siberian crane occupies that precarious position. The red-crowned crane population is currently estimated at 1,200 to 1,500.

Left: The hooded crane, revered and studied in Japan. Above: The red-crowned crane, classified as "vulnerable."

SARUS CRANE

Towering over all other cranes, the sarus stands as tall as six feet, and males weigh about 16 pounds. The sarus has four main resident flocks. One flock graces India and Nepal; one resides in Cambodia and Vietnam; two are located in northern Australia. These are tall grey birds with black secondaries and bright red heads and throats. The crown is pale green. Sarus cranes are among the least social of cranes, becoming so aggressive when nesting that zoos must isolate them.

In India, the sarus is considered sacred and thrives as a protected animal. Not much is known about the Indo-Chinese flock. In Australia, sarus cranes seem to be more successful than the smaller brolga cranes found in the same habitat. Expanding human populations are pressuring this species, although the increasing international cooperation among crane enthusiasts offers reason for hope.

The sarus crane, a six-footer.

SIBERIAN CRANE

The Siberian crane cannot be mistaken for anything else. A white bird with black primaries, the Siberian has an odd red face patch that begins with the bill and stops just behind the eyes. The longish bill curves downward. The face is slightly comical, resembling that of the booby. Researchers think the Siberian is closely related to Africa's wattled crane, because of similarities in the voice and in the performance of the unison call (a special pair-bonding behavior). The Siberian is a large crane—a male can weigh over 17 pounds. It breeds in the extreme north of Siberia. One flock winters in Iran, another in India, and a third winters along the Yangtze River in China.

Because the Siberian makes the longest migration of any crane in the world, it's exposed to many hazards each year. The west Asian flock is especially endangered. Much about this bird is simply not yet known, but

The Siberian crane: A face that's slightly comical.

researchers are working quickly to acquire information that can help Siberian cranes as they move into a threatening future.

WATTLED CRANE

The large wattled crane has a dark grey body set off by light grey wings. The feathered forehead is grey, and a prominent whitish wattle dangles below the base of the bill. White surrounds the head and continues down the neck to cover the breast and part of the shoulders. Wattled cranes are fiercely territorial. They don't bother to conceal their large nests, apparently because they defend the nests so capably. Males weigh 18 pounds. These cranes share the feeding habits of the Siberian crane.

The wattled is Africa's most endangered crane. Agriculture has eliminated much of its former habitat in South Africa, Botswana, Mozambique, and Zambia. The species is thought to number about 11,000 individuals, and its future is a matter of active concern.

WHITE-NAPED CRANE

The white-naped crane has a grey body set off by a naked red face and crown. A white patch covers the chin and rear of the head, carrying on down the back of the neck. The neck is white on top, grey below. These cranes nest along the Soviet Union's extreme eastern border with Manchuria and in Mongolia. They winter in a number of scattered locations, including China's Yangtze River, the demilitarized zone between North and South Korea, and Japan's island of Kyushu. Males weigh about 13 pounds.

The white-naped is losing habitat to agricultural development. Scientists need to know more about the migration routes the and specific regions of habitat required to bolster this bird's numbers. Officially classed as "vulnerable," the white-naped is an uncommon bird whose population is declining.

Left: The fiercely territorial wattled crane. Above: An uncommon crane, the white-naped.

WHOOPING CRANE

Whoopers are stately white birds with black primaries and red foreheads. The whooping crane's haunting, resonant bugle results from one of the longest windpipes in the bird world. These birds have proven less adaptable than sandhills. They're more dependent on marshes, and they're less able to take advantage of the nutritional windfall of human crops. Whooper males weigh over 17 pounds, making them one of the three largest cranes in the world.

To the beautiful whooping crane has gone the unhappy distinction of being America's most famous endangered species since just before World War II. From a high of over 1,200 birds in the 19th century, the population fell to 19 individuals by 1945. The latter decades of the 19th century were particularly disastrous. Whooping cranes lost a great deal of marshland habitat during this time—their nests were robbed by egg collectors, and many birds were shot for taxidermy mounts. When wildlife managers realized how seriously threatened the whoopers were, they quickly bought land for a refuge on the cranes' wintering ground. Aransas National Wildlife Refuge on the southeastern Texas Gulf Coast has protected the wintering whoopers ever since, although the refuge itself is considered threatened by oil spills. The search for the whooping crane's breeding grounds was more of a challenge, almost as dramatic as the search for the headwaters of the Nile. Ultimately, the nesting grounds were located in Wood Buffalo Park within Canada's Northwest Territories, an area already under protection. The whoopers migrating from Aransas to Wood Buffalo Park stop along the Platte River each spring.

The "cross-fostering" program, which involved sandhill cranes, has produced mixed results. Whooping crane eggs placed under sandhill mothers have hatched and survived. But because their adopted mothers are not whooping cranes, the young whoopers raised this way have not mated normally. More whooping cranes are alive today because of this program, yet the breeding success of these cranes has actually declined. The actual number of wild-bred whooping cranes has not changed significantly in five decades. There are now several captive breeding centers, plus one free, migrating flock. In spite of energetic and expensive preservation efforts, whooping cranes number only slightly over 220 individuals. The figures are not reassuring, and this beautiful bird remains gravely endangered.

The whooping crane, America's most endangered species.

APPENDIX B:
MORE ABOUT SANDHILLS

BOOKS ABOUT CRANES

There are a number of excellent publications on cranes in general and on sandhills in particular.

Anyone interested in sandhills should read Aldo Leopold's "Marshland Elegy," in the Wisconsin section of his classic *A Sand County Almanac*. Leopold wasn't *always* a great writer, but sandhills inspired him to what might be his most eloquent prose. Leopold genuinely feared that sandhills might be drifting toward extinction. It's regrettable that he didn't live long enough to see their numbers rise again in Wisconsin. *A Sand County Almanac* is sold in virtually every bookstore in North America.

There are three sandhill books.

The original book about sandhills is Lawrence H. Walkinshaw's *The Sandhill Cranes*. It's out of print, but can still be found in many libraries. Published in 1949, Walkinshaw's pioneering work is dated, of course, but still sound. Walkinshaw wrote at a time when researchers needed to accumulate a body of accurate data about crane movements, bird anatomy, and so forth. This book was written for researchers rather than the general public.

A more accessible book is Paul A. Johnsgard's *Those of the Grey Wind*. Johnsgard is a prominent naturalist and professor at the University of Nebraska. In this book, he follows a flock of lesser

A sandhill wades with white ibis.

sandhills from New Mexico to Alaska and back home. But as the birds move through space, they also move through time—moving, in fact, from 1860 to 1980. Johnsgard's strong, anti-hunting sentiments might bother some readers. This $5.95 publication from the University of Nebraska can be ordered from any bookstore.

An even more entertaining book is Dayton O. Hyde's *Sandy*. Hyde is a rancher and writer with a stubbornly independent mind and a keen eye for wildlife behavior. He's sensitive to the individual characters of animals, and *Sandy* tells the story of several cranes that lived with Hyde as pets. The book contains useful perceptions on sandhills, though it's mainly a ripping good story. The $12.95 paperback is published by Lyons & Burford, and can be ordered at any bookstore.

The best introduction to the wider world of cranes is a publication put together by the International Crane Foundation. *Reflections: The Story of Cranes* is short enough to be inexpensive, and yet the page size is expansive enough to do justice to some stunning photographs. The engaging text by Gretchen Holstein Schoff presents information about the 15 crane species, discussing the status of each. Mixed in are insights into cranes that could only come from the ICF. The price is $11.95 for the book and shipping costs; Wisconsin residents pay $.40 more for tax. Available from the ICF (address to follow).

For a more detailed and scholarly treatment of the same topic, the best book is Paul Johnsgard's *Cranes of the World*. Published in 1983, this book updates and extends an earlier monograph by Walkinshaw. *Cranes of the World* is now probably the most important text for serious fans of the world's cranes. The first section discusses key issues in the general biology of cranes. The bulk of the text presents detailed information on each of the world's species. Serious crane enthusiasts will want this summation of crane scholarship for their own libraries. The 258-page hardcover can be ordered from bookstores, and sells for about $40.00.

The prolific Johnsgard has written yet another crane book, which will be published in 1992. It strikes a middle ground between the two Johnsgard titles mentioned above. *Crane Music: A Natural History of North American Cranes* is both attractively written and informative. The emphasis is on sandhills and whooping cranes, though other species are treated. The new $19.95 hardcover book from The Smithsonian Press will be available from any bookstore following its publication.

A *Flight of Cranes*, by Dorothea Hayward Scott, is a slim but appealing volume about the mythology of cranes. The subtitle pretty much describes it:

"Stories and Poems from Around the World About Cranes." A $3.95 (shipping and handling included) paperback, this book is available from the ICF. All of the proceeds go to the Foundation.

Two books deal specifically with the Platte River.

Migratory Bird Habitat on the Platte and North Platte Rivers in Nebraska is a special, in-depth publication by one of the foremost conservation organizations working for the river, the Platte River Whooping Crane Trust. Copies sell for $11 postpaid, and are available directly from the Trust (address follows).

History fans will relish *The Great Platte River Road* by Merrill J. Mattes. This 521-page paperback won three awards for western history writing. Mattes spent years reading every existing journal, letter, and book written by pioneers, then patiently reassembled the most interesting of their comments in a comprehensible order. He weaves the emigrants' comments together, while keeping himself in the background. History is rarely this likable. The $15.95 paperback from the University of Nebraska Press can be ordered in any bookstore.

MAGAZINES AND BROCHURES

The May 1989 issue of *Audubon* magazine was devoted to the Platte River and its sandhills. Even by the high standards of the magazine when Les Line was its editor, this issue was outstanding. Five articles relate to the Platte and its cranes. Be sure to read John G. Mitchell's history piece and Suzanne Winckler's patient discussion of the water rights controversy. As always, the photography is superb. Sorry, back issues have been sold out; look for this issue in a library.

The Nebraska Game and Parks Commission offers a short, informative, and readable brochure called *Sandhill Cranes: Wings Over the Platte*. The brochure includes excellent text by Jon Farrar, plus wonderful photography by Farrar and others. The brochure is available at no cost from the Game and Parks Commission, Box 30370, Lincoln, Nebraska 68503.

VIDEOTAPES

At this time, there is one videotape about cranes on the market. *A Place for Whooping Cranes* was produced by Dave Erickson. In the VHS format, this tape sells for $22.95 (shipping and handling included; Wisconsin residents should add $1.00 for tax). You can order it through the ICF bookstore.

AUDIOTAPES

Nothing matches the experience of sharing a sunset with the sandhills of the Platte River, but one audiotape makes a good effort. The tape is narrated strictly by sandhill cranes; no announcer butts in to tell you what you are hearing. Try listening to this tape through stereo headphones with all the lights turned out. Imagine that you are camping out along the Platte several centuries ago. This $8.95 cassette is sold directly by the Stewards of the Platte (address follows), with discounts to members. The organization sells other products as well, among them sandhill t-shirts, pins, etc. Ask for the product brochure.

For a broader-spectrum sampler of waterfowl voices, listen to *Migration Music*, a NorthWord Press audiotape that includes the sounds of sandhill cranes, Canada geese, tundra swans, great blue herons, loons, songbirds, ducks, and more. The tape sells for $9.95, and can be ordered by calling NorthWord's toll-free number, 1-800-336-5666.

CRANE-WATCHING

The two key areas for watching sandhills are the Big Bend stretch of the Platte River in spring and the Jasper-Pulaski Game Management Area in fall. There are many other places where sandhills can be seen, but not in such spectacular numbers. Contact the appropriate departments of natural resources or local Audubon groups for guidance.

Several groups conduct or assist with tours on the Platte each March.

For current information, try any of the following numbers:

- ◆ Wings Over the Platte: 800-658-3178.

- ◆ Platte River Whooping Crane Trust: 308-384-4633.

- ◆ Lillian Annette Rowe Sanctuary: 308-468-5282.

- ◆ Nebraska Game and Parks: 402-464-0641.

- ◆ Kearney Chamber of Commerce: 308-237-3101.

The two largest programs are run by Grand Island (Wings Over the Platte) and Kearney (Crane Train). Wings Over the Platte is a three-day gathering featuring guided crane-watching tours, tours to the nearby Rainwater Basin, seminars, wildlife art, and a banquet. The Crane Train is a bus tour that makes several stops along the river. Tour guides explain the significance of special features.

The two groups that maintain blinds for daybreak and sunset crane-watching are the Platte River Trust and the Audubon Society's Rowe Sanctuary. Blind space is limited, however, and cannot accommodate all interested parties at times. You might inquire about the possibility of making reservations.

Here are some Platte crane-watching tips:

◆ Most visitors come at the wrong time. Either they come as early as possible, when cranes are especially spooky and the weather is often marginal, or they want to experience the peak, when the human crowds are as large as they get. The early cranes come in mid-February. The peak falls in the third week of March. Unless you want to participate in one of the organized programs, schedule your trip before or after the peak.

◆ The best time to crane-watch is in early April. There are fewer crane tourists around at that time, and the sandhills are more easily approached, because they've become accustomed to crane-watchers.

◆ Getting great crane photos is a challenge. Bring a tripod and a tele-photo lens of at least 4X power (200mm lens for a 35mm camera).

◆ It's sometimes possible to get good pictures from the blinds, though the cranes don't spend much time on the river when light levels are sufficient for photography.

◆ At any period during the crane sea-son, the best time to observe the sandhills is mid-week. You'll avoid the crowds and get better chances at a blind seat. The cranes might be more approachable, too, if they haven't been pressured for a day or two.

◆ For daytime crane-watching, bring binoculars or, better, a spotting scope.

◆ Please respect private property and the cranes' need for security.

Jasper-Pulaski's fall concentration does not feature quite as many cranes as the spring Platte congregation, but 14,000 sandhills make for a stunning spectacle. Beyond four or five thousand cranes, it ceases to matter how many birds you're seeing.

These are greater sandhills, the largest sub-type. They are reportedly less wary than the Platte's sandhills, possibly because they haven't been hunted for decades. These birds provide fewer crane-watching opportunities during the day than the Platte birds, because they mostly feed inside the management area on "lure crops" planted for them.

Cranes start showing up there in September. The peak comes in mid to late October. The Indiana Department of Natural Resources maintains a large, high platform blind for crane-watchers. The trail leading to the blind offers a self-guided nature walk and many sta-tions where visitors are informed about the life history of cranes.

For more information, contact the Indiana Audubon Society at its Mary Gray Bird Sanctuary: 317-825-9788.

CONSERVATION GROUPS

The premier crane conservation group is, of course, the International Crane Foundation (ICF). They have an attractive quarterly publication, *The Bugle*, that presents current activities and the very latest in crane research. Membership rates begin at $20 for individuals. Write to the ICF at E-11376 Shady Lane Road, Baraboo, WI 53913 or call 608-356-9462.

The Platte River Whooping Crane Trust does not solicit members at this time, though it may do so in the future. The Trust is spearheading important efforts to save the Platte and its cranes, working both in the political arena and through important research projects. The group maintains a section of river roosting habitat that is extremely popular with people and cranes. Anyone who wants to be on its mailing list will receive a quarterly newsletter at no charge, though the Trust hopes that most people will make a donation to cover the shipping and mailing costs. Write to them at 2550 North Diers Avenue, Suite H, Grand Island, NE 68803. A unique Trust program allows friends of the Platte to "adopt" an acre of crane habitat for $500.

The Stewards of the Platte is a newer group co-founded by Lonnie Logan and Dick Placzek. The intention of the Stewards is to serve as common ground for all parties that are contending for control of the Platte. While firmly committed to preserving the Platte's unique qualities, the Stewards of the Platte organization hopes to increase dialogue and mutual respect. Annual membership starts at $20, and members receive a quarterly newsletter. Write to them at Box 2201, Grand Island, NE 68802.

Several national conservation organizations are working to protect the Platte. Foremost is the Audubon Society, which has been fighting expensive and complicated legal battles. Others actively involved include the Sierra Club, the National Wildlife Federation, the American Rivers Council, and the Nature Conservancy.